M000078143

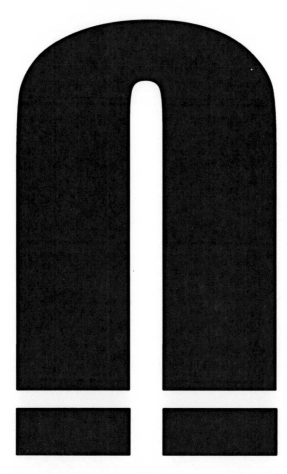

MAGNETIC™
SPONSORING

MAGNETIC SPONSORING
ISBN 978-1-6196129-3-8

www.magneticsponsoring.com
www.mikedillard.com

LIONCREST
PUBLISHING

www.lioncrest.com

CONTENTS

BONUS TRAINING VIDEO

"What To Do Next..."

I've put together a private video tutorial just
for Magnetic Sponsoring book owners that
will help you apply these powerful marketing
strategies in your business as fast as possible.

You can get access to this free training video at:

WWW.MAGNETICSPONSORING.COM/BONUS

Introduction

Well, hello there...

My name is Mike Dillard, and welcome to *Magnetic Sponsoring*™.

I was 24 years old when I first wrote this book as a training manual for my personal downline.

Copies of it quickly leaked to other teams and leaders in the industry. Most of the old-school guys cursed it as sacrilege when they could find the time between their hotel meetings.

The rest of the industry asked me if they could buy copies for their team. Some leaders even made it required reading for their prospects before they'd sponsor them.

At this point, I've lost count of how many 100,000+ copies have been sold over the years, but what I do remember are the thousands of success stories that people have sent in, and the faces of those who've shaken my hand and said "thank you" when our paths crossed in person.

I wish I could reach out and shake your hand right now. I wish I could tell you how excited I am for you because I know your world and your approach to network marketing are about to change forever.

While this book represents a single stepping-stone along your path to freedom, it has come to represent a very special part of my legacy.

So, most of all, I wish to say thank you for providing me with the privilege and opportunity to make a positive impact on your life.

Thank you for your leadership,

MIKE DILLARD

Here's what you're going to learn today...

If you're brand new to the industry and you're not really sure where to start, this book will allow you to sidestep years of ridiculous marketing tactics, like cold-calling, buying leads, posting fliers, putting stickers on your car, or spamming the Internet, and provide you with a proven blueprint for a successful business.

If you're trying to build your business on a budget like I had to, *Magnetic Sponsoring* will teach you how to get paid to prospect. This will allow you to generate as many high-quality leads as you want, as long as you want, for free.

No matter how good you are, when it comes to sponsoring new distributors, 90 percent of your prospects will never join your business, which means you're missing out on 90 percent of your potential revenue. Here in *Magnetic Sponsoring*, I'll teach you how to successfully flip those numbers around, allowing you to make money whether someone joins your business or not.

If you're shy and hate the idea of selling anything to anyone, don't worry. I was, too. This book will teach you attraction marketing strategies that will have distributors and customers approaching you with credit card in hand, ready to buy.

If you want to learn how to make money on demand, I'll teach you how I used these *Magnetic Sponsoring* strategies to make over $3.2 million in just *seven days*.

If you lack personal confidence and wonder why your prospects don't take you or your business seriously, don't worry. I spent a good six years in your shoes until I figured out the concepts of personal attraction and leadership that I'm going to teach you today.

If you're wondering if these strategies are outdated, they aren't. The bigger and louder the world and the Internet gets, the more effective *Magnetic Sponsoring* strategies become.

If you're wondering if you can apply these strategies to any kind of business, in any kind of industry, you can. In fact, they were created in the traditional business world, outside multi-level marketing (MLM). I simply brought them into this industry.

Now before we begin, I'd like to set some expectations. Specifically, what you can expect from me and from this book…

First and foremost, my loyalty is to you. As an aspiring entrepreneur, you want to improve your lot in life and the end goal you desire is financial freedom.

My loyalty is not to "the industry" and it is not to a particular method of building a business. I believe the only right way to build a business is the way that's right for you.

One of my biggest pet peeves in network marketing is that the leadership tries to force everyone in their downline into a specific methodology for building a business, under the guise of "duplication."

Well, this may come as a surprise, but it turns out that all of us have different personalities and different strengths.

I spent six years trying to force myself into the molds provided by my upline. As a result, failure persisted.

I thought I was broken; that I had a problem that needed to be fixed.

And then I realized that I was simply a different person. The individuals who fit into that mold were social extroverts who loved talking to people in person and at meetings. I was an introvert who shuddered at the thought.

The moment that I allowed myself the freedom to build this business in a manner that catered to my strengths, instead of trying to change myself to fit theirs, I had massive success.

So, is *Magnetic Sponsoring* the definitive book when it comes to building a network marketing business?

Absolutely not. And neither is any other book.

Amway is still the 500-pound gorilla in the industry, earning over $10 billion in annual sales. They do not allow Internet marketing of any kind. All they use is 100 percent old-school warm market methods.

Clearly it's effective, but that strategy does not fit my personality or my interests. If that's how I had to build this business, I would have left the industry.

Find the methods that are aligned with you and your personality. Only then will you get the results you desire.

Now, before we dive into the nitty-gritty, I wanted to share a few things about myself with you that I believe many of you will find important.

First of all, I want you to know that *everyone* sucks at this industry in the beginning.

The biggest gift network marketing has to offer you is that it will instantly make you aware of your weaknesses, and then unapologetically require you to address them.

My early sponsors neglected to tell me that in the beginning. It appeared as if their businesses had been all sunshine and rainbows since day one.

I believe most leaders in this industry tend to skip over the war stories of their career because they're afraid you'll run away screaming if you actually knew what they went through to achieve success.

Looking back, I wish that my upline mentors would have shared their stories of struggle with me. If they had, it would have made the challenges I faced along my journey that much easier to swallow.

In many ways, we are all part of a very special brotherhood, united by the battle scars we earn during this amazing process of growth.

Let me share mine with you…

I got started in this industry during my freshman year in college:

I was extremely shy, had very little self-confidence, and was dead broke. I wondered how anyone older than me could possibly take me seriously. After all, what the hell did a broke 20-year-old know about making money and business?

I was the guy who would drive his upline mad with endless questions, and then do whatever I could to avoid calling my prospects. For some reason, when it came time to pick up the phone and call my leads, an unexpected trip to Office Depot for a new headset or whiteboard was always on order.

The only people I sponsored during my first five or six years were family members and relatives.

Yes, I did lose friends because of my insistent pursuit.

I was the dude driving the crappy car on my way to my crappy job, with my business opportunity sticker plastered across the back of the window.

I hung fliers on my college campus. I dropped "sizzle cards" in strip mall parking lots at midnight, and was chased off by security.

Once I overcame my fear of the phone (long story), I bought genealogy lists and cold-called 300 people per day.

I spent every spare dollar I had on opportunity leads.

I lived in an empty apartment, furnished with nothing more than a mattress and my desk, for years after college.

And, of course, I joined at least 12 different companies in a five-year span, because failing in one just wasn't good enough.

And then one day, everything changed...

After six years of failure, I stumbled upon the marketing wisdom I'm going to teach you here today in this book.

Within 18 months, I went from broke and waiting tables to making my first million dollars.

My fears disappeared and sponsoring new distributors became effortless.

I went on to build the largest residual income check in my last opportunity, selling a product that sold for $5,000 to $20,000 each.

I built the largest social networking site in the MLM industry, which became one of the top 2,500 websites in the world, with over one million pages of user-submitted content indexed by Google.

I grew *Magnetic Sponsoring* into a publishing company that's produced more than $25 million in revenue.

Since then, I've moved on to build a financial education company that produced $10 million in revenue in its first 12 months.

I've built a list of more than **one million** email subscribers.

And my work has been knocked-off, swiped, and emulated for a decade. It has created dozens of other networking "gurus" you've heard of who have essentially re-written and re-packaged what they learned here.

Which should leave you with one question…

What in the world happened during that 18-month window that made such a startling difference?

Well, you're about to find out. Let's get started…

CHAPTER ONE

How to Become the Hunted, Instead of the Hunter

After years of failure, I'd finally started to sponsor people on a consistent basis each month, but it was a brutal process.

I'd call the leads I'd purchased, take them through a basic interview process, and then send them more information online, or schedule a three-way call with my upline.

If I made a sale, I might have pocketed $100.

The rest of my time was spent training and motivating those new people to do the same thing.

I'd fought so hard for so many years to reach this point, and now that I had, the reality was a hard pill to swallow.

If this was what my life would be like as a professional network marketer for the next 20 years, I wanted nothing to do with it.

The part that I hated the most was the constant, never-ending pursuit of calling and sponsoring new distributors.

So I said to myself, "If I could only get 5 to 10 people to contact me every day about my business, I'd have it made, and this business would be fun!"

How great would it be if 10 people called you up every single day, ready and excited to join your team? Their questions already answered, objections met, and costs explained. All you needed to do was sign them up and plug them into the training process.

I needed to figure out how to become the hunted, instead of the hunter.

Which left me with one very important question...

So how do you get people to contact and pursue you?

- What makes a person attractive to others?
- Why do groupies flock irrationally to celebrities and rock stars?
- Why do people become "famous"?
- Why do some women find certain men completely irresistible even if they're dead broke, and usually jerks?
- Why can you throw 10 complete strangers in a group together and, within minutes, a leader will emerge that the others will follow?
- Why does everyone want to work with the top earners in a company?
- Why can those individuals join any opportunity in the world and have a sizable organization within weeks or months, with little or no effort compared to the average Joe who's busting

his tail for dismal results?
- And, most of all, how do you tap into this phenomenon and become pursued yourself?

The answer lies in basic human psychology, so that's where we need to start.

What I'm about to share with you is at the core of human-to-human attraction.

The first thing you need to understand is that *attraction is not a choice.*

It's a biological/instinctual trigger that evolved millions of years ago to help keep you alive, which is usually why it's never consciously understood or perceived by people until they actually start to study it.

Here's a very basic historical illustration: By nature, people thrive and live in social groups. They follow a leader until they gain enough experience and confidence to challenge for leadership themselves or start their own group.

This is a survival instinct that has been ingrained in us.

People cannot survive on their own, so we've formed tribes and families.

The leader (usually referred to as the *Alpha*) is typically the strongest and most dominant individual in the group or family, both physically and mentally. One of his primary responsibilities is to protect his group, and, in return for that protection, they follow him.

That instinct is still present and definitely used today, but the inherent value of a leader is now expressed through different abilities such as business savvy, sociability, monetary means, and education, instead of physical prowess.

Essentially, we are hard-wired to find other people attractive or unattractive based on the level of value they have to offer, because we gain a portion of their power/value *through association*.

Think of a celebrity and his or her entourage.

The people in their group gain social status through their association with him or her, making them more attractive to others. They become "cooler" and more attractive to other people outside the group who want in.

There are two important lessons here:

1. People have a subconscious attraction to others who convey leadership qualities and have a high level of personal value.
2. If you want to make it big in networking (or anything in life), you must learn to convey those qualities and eventually become a leader with value to offer others.

If your prospect or new distributor doesn't have these qualities, they will struggle as well until they develop them. It's likely that this process will continue for years until they finally gain the right qualities by accident, or until some nice person like you happens to share this book with them.

Now when it comes to network marketing, and sponsoring specifically, there's one key concept you must understand:

People do not join a business; they join YOU.

You see, there are basically three categories of people in life: *Alphas,*

Pre-Alphas, and *Betas*.

You can also think of these as *Established Leaders, Up-and-Coming Leaders,* and *Followers*, respectively. Each category offers exclusive benefits and abilities, or lack-there-of, to the individuals within them.

So which one of our three categories are you in right now?

Here's a simple, but very effective test you can take immediately...

Next time you're out in public and you make eye contact with an attractive person of the opposite sex, notice when you break eye contact with them.

Did you look down and away first, or did they?

If you looked away first, you likely have a Beta or Pre-Alpha state of mind. If you held the gaze until they looked away, you're probably an Alpha.

Then, ask yourself if you're worried about what that person thought of you. Did you wonder what they were thinking? Were you concerned about being judged? If so, then you're in a Beta or Pre-Alpha mindset.

Well, here's the interesting part: The group you're in is determined not by money, experience, the job you have, or anything else for that matter.

It's determined by your state of mind, which is not given or bestowed upon you by others. Rather, your group reflects your personal beliefs about yourself.

You, and only you, decide which of these three categories you are in.

Society will either agree with you and comply, or will chastise you for being a "poser," depending upon *whether or not your actions are congruent with your beliefs.*

This is called your "frame," or state of mind.

You cannot fake belief. You cannot pretend or act. You truly believe you are or you are not. In the coming pages, I'll teach you how to genuinely increase your personal value so you can be truly more valuable to others.

You will likely feel like a "poser" when you start to adopt and accept a new belief system about yourself. You will likely get "caught" by an Alpha prospect who can sense that you're not being genuine yet. But that's the key word… *yet.*

That's what people talk about when they mention "fake it until you make it." Faking it does not mean lying; it simply means that you're going to struggle a bit as you go through the process of moving from a follower to an up-and-coming leader, and eventually to a recognized leader.

It's similar to that awkward period in middle school, when you're not quite a child or an adult.

Your friends, family members, and coworkers will challenge your new view of yourself. That's why there's always animosity and resentment in an office environment when someone gets promoted from a worker to a management/leadership position.

Challenging your current views about yourself and acting like a different person is a scary, yet wonderfully rewarding activity.

Increasing your value to others and taking the initiative to move yourself from one group to another is what personal development is all about.

EVERY leader has been there, and you need to know this… Belief always comes before results.

Belief leads to certain actions and behaviors. Those actions and behaviors are going to be awkward in the beginning, but given dedication, time, and affirmation, those actions and behaviors will turn you into the type of person you need to be in order to generate the results you seek.

Your goal in the network marketing industry is to become what I call an "Alpha Networker™."

An example of an Alpha would be a successful upline leader *living in a mindset of abundance,* and who is pursued and followed by others.

An example of a Pre-Alpha would be someone who's recently started to push their comfort zone when it comes to expressing leadership. This is where the struggle is found before the big reward.

- They've started training their new distributors and providing them with instructions.
- Their posture on the phone with prospects has become more authoritative.
- They've started hosting and introducing guests on training calls.
- They've taken personal responsibility for their lead generation and marketing campaigns.
- Their level of personal confidence and self-worth has begun to rise significantly.

The third group consists of Betas. They typically have very little confidence or value to offer others, so they simply flock to those who do have it in hopes that it will rub off.

They are essentially "unsure" of themselves or still uncomfortable with the idea of being a leader. They typically live life in a state of "reaction," where life events and other people dictate their rules and reality. Everything is usually someone else's fault.

The primary difference between Pre-Alphas and Betas is that Pre-Alphas have the vision, courage, and willingness to lead themselves through adversity and challenge. If you cannot first lead yourself through struggles, how can you expect others to eventually follow you?

With that said, there are two important pieces of information to note: one cannot exist without the other, and everyone must follow before they can lead. It took me six years to move from a Beta to a Pre-Alpha to an Alpha.

The bottom line is that in order to trigger attraction in others, you need to be an Alpha in all aspects of life, but especially when it comes to business.

Here are common personality traits shared by Alphas:

- Alphas are leaders who are naturally attractive because they radiate confidence and are not concerned with outside criticism.
- They know exactly what they want and focus their energies on achieving their goals.
- They have a frame so strong that people are sucked into their reality. Everything they do reflects the rules of what is possible and what is not inside that reality.
- They tend to have a lot of rules that you must follow when

you are around them.
- They treat themselves with integrity and they absolutely will not tolerate disrespect; in fact, they punish it, usually by ignoring the person, or removing them from their life.

Quite a few people have found out that I work this way, as do Dan Kennedy, Perry Marshall, and Yanik Silver.

(Have you ever seen how Donald Trump answers an ignorant or disrespectful question? He doesn't. Period. He either ignores it or provides an answer to the question he feels he should have been asked in the first place.)

- They offer tremendous amounts of value to others.
- They truly love themselves.
- They love and protect those who matter to them.
- They always radiate positive energy and optimism.
- They respect themselves and their bodies, dressing with style and living healthy lifestyles.
- They do what the majority is unwilling to.

The upline leader with a team of 10,000 is an Alpha. The guy you know who gets the hottest girls is an Alpha. The woman you admire on stage, dressed with class, dignity, and style is an Alpha. The guy in the Ferrari at the light next to you doesn't give a crap about what you or anyone else thinks of him. He's an Alpha. The pastor at your church is an Alpha. The woman who throws the party where everyone wants to be is an Alpha.

And in the particular case of network marketing, an Alpha is the person who sponsors people effortlessly.

The differences between Alphas and Betas in lifestyle, income, social circles, opportunity, respect, and admiration are vast.

Alphas get the guy or girl, the car, the respect, the money, and have more opportunities in life to impact more people in a positive manner, whether it's through public service, creating a charitable foundation, instructing, mentorship, etc.

When you're an Alpha Networker, you offer value and prospects automatically pursue an association with you so they can share a little piece of that power and value.

This is the *foundational concept* of *Magnetic Sponsoring*.

The Alpha Networker doesn't need to make follow-up calls or court prospects. They don't need to answer questions about their income, or convince anyone of anything because their previous reputation and results speak for them.

Their business thrives in a constant state of abundance, where many times they will need to actually limit the new number of distributors they sponsor, or hand them down to one of their group leaders because they simply don't have the time to work with so many people themselves.

I've been in that position many times. Would you like to be there as well?

Of course you would.

Actually… you don't have a choice.

Successful network marketers, by definition, are Alpha. A multi-level compensation plan which requires you to build and lead an organization mandates that trait by default.

Take some time to think about this information and how it relates to where you're at in your current state of personal development.

This business is 90 percent mental and 10 percent execution because when you're an Alpha (a state of mind), everything else naturally and automatically flows TO YOU, and any past struggles and roadblocks fade away.

All of this naturally leads us to the question, "How do you become an Alpha Networker?"

Simple...

You need to genuinely increase your sense of self-worth, and the best way to do that is to increase your value to the world by learning new skills.

So, here's the cold hard truth...

The amount of money you make today is a direct reflection of your PVL, or "Personal Value Level."

Human society uses a simple tool called "money" to quickly and easily communicate the relative value of all things, from an apple, to a gallon of gasoline, to the wage for a job.

Through our free-market system, the world dictates how much money you make according to three factors:

1. The number of people who are also capable of performing a particular job (competition).
2. The amount of specialized skills or education needed to perform the job (education).
3. The number of people around the world that your work benefits (leverage).

For example, there are two reasons why restaurant waiters, janitors, or retail workers make so little.

As a waiter:

1. There is an almost endless supply of workers who can fill your position.
2. Waiting tables does not require rare, specialized skills or education.
3. You're only serving a dozen people at any given time, which means you have very little leverage.

So, if you're in one of these positions, your PVL to the world is very low, which is why you'd be making very little money.

On the other hand, brain surgeons make around $1 million per year because:

1. There are very few qualified individuals in the world that are able to perform the task.
2. The work requires extremely specialized knowledge and skills.
3. You can only perform brain surgery on one person at a time, so there is no way to benefit the masses.

Now, the reason they make around $1 million per year, instead of $20 million, is because they're missing piece number three... **leverage**.

Now, please don't take any of this personally or get offended if you feel like you have a low personal value level right now.

I'm simply stating a truth that I've learned through personal experience that most people would be too politically correct to talk about.

But until you understand WHY some people make more than others, there's no way you can break free and *choose* a more lucrative path.

Now, let's compare these two examples to what I did through my first company, *Magnetic Sponsoring*...

My *Magnetic Sponsoring* courses teach individuals and small business owners how to market and sell their products more effectively online.

1. Are there many people who can write these books based on years of personal experience?

No.

There are only a few hundred people here in the US who have successfully sold more than $50 million in products online from a home business.

2. Does online marketing require specialized skills?

Yes.

These skills are not taught in school and can only be learned by those who proactively seek out this kind of training.

3. Does this business provide me with the ability to impact the masses?

Yes.

If I were teaching people how to market online, one-on-one over the phone, or in person, I'd have zero leverage.

Because I sell books and videos, which can be mass-produced and distributed to an infinite number of people around the world, I have an infinite amount of leverage.

As you can see, my job waiting tables had a very low PVL to the world, where my job as a modern day educator using technology to reach the masses has a very high PVL.

One job pays $30,000 per year. The other job pays millions per year. The number of hours worked in either case is the same.

HOW DO YOU INCREASE YOUR PVL?

The fastest way to reach the incredible levels of success you want to achieve is to increase your value to the world. And the fastest way to increase your value to the world is to acquire new skills.

The biggest mistake I made during my six years of failure was that I was looking for something outside of myself to bring me results.

I was looking for a marketing system or a traffic gimmick of some kind that would make me rich.

The simple truth of the matter is that I didn't have any value to offer the world.

My network marketing opportunity is all I had, and that opportunity had no real value.

There were thousands of other distributors in the same company that my prospects could have joined. And then there are thousands of other network marketing companies they could have pursued.

People had no reason to join my team over any other because I had no unique value or skills to offer them.

My big breakthrough finally came when I discovered that acquiring new skills is the only way to increase your value to others and to the world.

And then something funny starts to happen as you learn these new skillsets.

You start to gain knowledge and abilities, which gives you confidence, and confidence is the path to Alpha status.

How do you know if you're moving in the right direction?

Simple… You'll start to adopt the qualities all Alphas share:

- You will start to adopt an abundance mentality. This is a core concept needed for success. Alphas never come from a "frame of need." You don't "need" to sponsor people. You don't "need" people to join you. When you "need" something from someone, you are automatically supplicating to them and giving them the power. If you don't have the power in a given situation, you're not the Alpha leader, are you? Any feelings of "need" are crushed by living in a frame or mindset of limitless abundance — abundance of money, abundance of prospects, abundance of opportunity, etc. When you live in abundance, you do not fear loss or failure.
- You are unconcerned with criticism. When you're an Alpha leader, some Betas will feel insecure and blame you for all of their problems. Many of them resent successful people. Betas do this because it's the only option available to them when they are unwilling to take responsibility for their own life's circumstances. As the saying goes, "Wolves do not concern

themselves with the opinions of sheep."

- You dictate the terms. You're not mean; you're assertive. If other people want to interact with you, it's on your terms. This is commonly called "posture" in the work-at-home arena.
- You are willing to say "no." You know you can't please everyone, but it does not matter because you live in a frame of abundance.
- As an Alpha, you give instructions just like the quarterback does or the head coach of a football team.
- You protect and serve those who follow you. Your goal is to uplift and improve the lives of those around you, not because you feel obligated, but because you want to.
- You respect yourself and your body, dressing with style and living a healthy lifestyle.
- You take risks, but once again recognize there really is no such thing as risk when you live in a mindset of abundance.
- As an Alpha Networker, you're confident, socially powerful, outgoing, fun, a leader, secure in yourself, filled with self-esteem, and are someone able to joke around with others and be playful.
- You have a strong physical presence. Alpha males are relaxed (watch 007), take up space with their shoulders, and always hold eye contact. Alpha females sit up straight, hold eye contact, and move with poise and purpose.
- You use a strong, confident voice and control the conversation. You tend to speak with a relaxed authority and aren't afraid to interrupt the other person.
- When a prospect questions or challenges anything about a Beta's product or opportunity, the Beta will get frustrated, defensive, and/or offended. They will immediately begin to seek the approval of the prospect. As an Alpha Networker, you take control of the situation before it happens, or simply ignore it.
- You never seek approval by ending sentences with "isn't it?" or "right?" These questions tacked onto the end of sentences

make you sound weak-willed, particularly if your vocal pitch rises. Right?

- You are extremely protective of your most valuable resource, which is your time, and do not give it away to others unless they deserve it.

After all of this is said and done, *Magnetic Sponsoring* and generating attraction is about ONE THING: Increasing your value to others and to the world.

Alphas are valuable people.

The more valuable you become to others, the more they will seek you out.

The more valuable you become to others, the more Alpha you will be.

That's THE secret to becoming magnetic.

Again, in order to become "magnetic," you must increase your value to others through education and experience.

Believing and knowing that you hold true value to other people gives you the confidence and the abundance mentality you need in order to become an Alpha Networker.

After realizing this, I became a man on a mission.

I spent every dime I could on information, courses, and books. I went out and learned marketing skills that others will be unwilling to learn and, in the process, I became extremely valuable to others.

Sit down and ask yourself these questions:

How do you bring value to the table right now in the eyes of your leads? Remember, your opportunity doesn't matter. There are thousands of opportunities. How do you PERSONALLY bring value to them?

Can you teach them how to advertise and generate leads? Are you great on the phone during three-way calls? Can you host killer meetings?

If you struggle with sponsoring, it's because you don't bring any true value to the table yet.

If someone is going to join you, they're looking to acquire some kind of power by associating themselves with you.

If they're not going to gain power of some kind by working with you, they won't work with you. They'll just go find a leader who will provide them with that advantage.

Now here's the great part: It doesn't take a lot to increase your value in the eyes of a prospect, because most don't have a clue when it comes to building a home business.

All you need to do is know just a little bit more than they do, and you're instantly in a position of power and value.

With that being said, let me share a really big pet-peeve of mine when it comes to acquiring value…

Specifically, it's when people send me questions like this:

"Is this course going to tell me everything I need to know, or am I just going to have to buy another book of yours after this?"

Or: "I've already bought dozens of books on this stuff and I'm still not successful. Why should I buy yours?"

They will never make it with this attitude and should go back to their job as quickly as possible. They are looking for a book, a tool, a widget, or something else outside themselves that will finally bring them success.

They don't understand that it's not about them or what they'll need to spend on another book. It's about increasing their value to others so that they may better serve more people.

What if I told you that every single year I spend $50,000 to $100,000 to further my education as an entrepreneur?

Would you believe it? Would it make sense to you, or is your jaw on the floor in disbelief?

Well, it's true. Between mastermind groups, events, and courses, I spend almost six figures per year just to maintain a high level of value to my customers.

I'm smart enough to invest in myself; to increase the value of Mike Dillard to the world, *because the more valuable I become to others, the more I am pursued.*

The fact that you're reading this course means that you understand this principle to some degree.

Don't stop now. INCREASE your pursuit of value-giving education.

Every single successful entrepreneur I know has studied and accumulated information on their industry extensively.

Without exception, those with the biggest bank accounts also have the biggest personal libraries, and they don't stop learning when they reach their goal. They do the opposite — just like I did. They start spending more. Much more.

This book is not the end of your education, it's the beginning. You will never find an "end-all, be-all" course that will teach you everything you need to know.

It does not exist and never will.

Only a Beta would seek out a magic lamp of some kind that promises to bring them what they desire.

When you're buying information, you're looking for just one good idea that you didn't have before. Just one. If that's all you get from a CD set, book, or course, you've gotten your money's worth because it all adds up over time.

Don't be afraid to spend *big* money on marketing courses either. I routinely buy CD and book sets or conference tickets that cost $1,000 to $5,000 each without hesitation because what I learn always ends up making me much more in the long run.

This attitude towards my education was a turning point in my career.

It's like a puzzle, and every new resource you expose yourself to adds a few more pieces.

Buy every single book you can get your hands on.

In the end, success in this industry comes down to just two things:

1. Becoming a leader to others by increasing your value.

2. Acquiring the ability to express your value to the world through marketing.

I can give you free leads all day long, but if you don't see yourself as a leader and express those qualities, you'll never sponsor any of them.

The greatest benefit this industry provides is not the money, the time, or even the friendships; it's what this industry can make of you — the "person you become."

We all come to the table with the same tools, marketing materials, and systems. You and the strengths you bring to the table are the only unknown factors in the equation.

Choosing the right company with the right product and the right marketing system can help you reach your goal *faster* — just as a sharp axe will out-perform a dull one — but it will not determine your end result!

My business took off once I decided to just simply "help others," even if I didn't know everything. I was going to try and help as many people as I could. I stopped worrying about the marketing plan, the presentation, and all of that stuff.

This is the key for most people who are stuck: they are focusing on things like tools, websites, and compensation plans too much, always looking for something outside themselves that will bring success. This is a Beta behavior.

Yet the desire to help people wasn't enough in and of itself. I had to learn how to market so I could get that message and that energy into the marketplace. Intentions are useless without the ability to execute them.

But how I market is quite different than anything you've ever seen before, and much, much more profitable...

So, let's dive into the fun stuff...

CHAPTER TWO

"You Inc." — How to Create a Real Business with Zero Competition

The "You Inc." concept was one of the most revolutionary aspects of this book when it was first released because it addressed the giant 10-ton gorilla sitting in every network marketer's living room for the very first time, in an uncomfortably honest fashion.

So what is "You Inc."?

Well it's the solution to a very big problem you currently have, but probably don't know about.

You Inc. is all about realizing that your business is much bigger than a MLM product or opportunity—which, in fact, is not real "businesses" at all.

That's right… Your Network Marketing business isn't actually a real business, and here's why…

A real "business" has several important characteristics:

1. A real business is bigger than any one product or company. If you have a single product or service, you don't have a business, you have an offer.
2. A real business cannot disappear or be taken away from you overnight. It has employees, contracts, and inventory.
3. In a real business you have control and ownership of a core asset.

So let's take a look at your MLM business.

As an independent distributor, you have zero control and zero ownership. You have a tentative contract with a networking company that can be ripped up at the drop of a hat, (and often is).

This industry likes to sell people on the idea that their downline is an asset "you own and can even will to your children."

Well let me be frank… That's 100 percent bullshit.

During my time in the MLM industry, I've seen dozens of successful leaders lose their distributorships for one reason or another.

Years of work and millions of dollars were taken away in an instant.

If you think your downline is your asset, you need to wake up and read your distributor agreement.

The company owns it. If you doubt that, try to recruit your downline away into another opportunity and see what happens (hint: you'll be sued).

The reality is that you are a 100 percent commission-based sales rep who owns NOTHING, and by definition, "nothing" can't be a business.

So how do you fix that?

Simple... You turn *yourself* into a business. You build "You Inc."

The skills that you've acquired to serve the needs of others or solve their problems and the relationships that you build by providing your value to the world become a real-life commodity that can be traded for money.

"I" as a person, and the services I can bring to others as an individual (like this book), became my business.

My knowledge, leadership, and expertise in marketing became my product.

The people who followed and consumed my work became my distribution channel.

The network marketing company I chose to promote to the people in my distribution channel became a single offer in the overall business model of "Mike Dillard Inc."

My downline or distributorship could disappear overnight and it wouldn't matter because the primary asset, and all of the real equity, was located within me, my name, and the relationships I held with the people I served in the marketplace.

Which means you and your business are now immune to outside circumstances and influences. No matter what happens in the marketplace, your business will remain intact and able to produce a profit as long as you want it to.

And here's another incredible benefit of a "You Inc." business:

The competition disappears forever.

Think about this for a minute…

Any successful network marketing company will have 50,000–1,000,000+ distributors. ALL OF THEM are marketing the exact same opportunity and the exact same products.

Not only do you have to compete with 1,000 other companies and opportunities in the market, but you also have to compete against the thousands of other distributors in your very company.

Sounds like a pretty crappy deal if you ask me.

But as you've probably started to understand, the strategies of *Magnetic Sponsoring* and You Inc. address that problem forever because you're no longer selling a product or an opportunity; you're selling yourself and the value you have to offer your team as a leader.

And guess what? There's only one of you in the entire world, which means you have zero competition.

I've often been asked if *Magnetic Sponsoring* still works considering I wrote the very first version back in 2005.

The answer is a resounding YES. And in fact, the bigger and louder the world gets, the more effective it becomes.

Why is that?

As someone who is providing value and leadership first, you stand out as an island of sanity. You become a voice of reason and a trusted advisor in a jungle filled with pitfalls and false promises.

As long as you hold yourself with integrity, people will tie their ship to yours and never let go, as you are a needle in the haystack of the home business world.

CHAPTER THREE

The Business Model I've Used to Make Over $50 Million

Now that you understand why attraction marketing works and the advantages of building a "You Inc." business, let's start to discuss the primary skill you'll need to make money in this business, or any other business: marketing.

The entire point of building a network marketing business is to create well-educated distributors who can market and acquire a large base of happy **product customers** who have nothing to do with the business. They just love and use the product, which creates a monthly residual income for you and your family.

The biggest problem I've seen develop over the last few years (primarily due to the Internet) is that this industry has focused entirely on building offers that cater to weakness. These are marketing websites and campaigns that promote a "we'll do all the work for you" mentality typically seen in "power line" or binary systems.

It makes perfect sense why that's happened from a marketing standpoint, and you will learn why in the upcoming chapters, but when it comes to building a network and developing leaders, catering to weakness is lethal.

I'll be honest... *Magnetic Sponsoring* will not determine your success. Thinking that anything outside yourself will determine the end result in your business and your life is ignorant and something only a Beta would think.

What *Magnetic Sponsoring* will do is empower a skilled business owner and let him or her achieve massive success faster and easier than ever through the application of correct strategies and tactics.

Most networkers are like homebuilders, except when they fail to build their house, they go back to the tool store and try a new hammer. When that doesn't work, they go do it again, and again, and again (like trying dozens of opportunities and lead companies).

If they would only realize it's the skill and knowledge of the person swinging the hammer that mattered, and not the company or the compensation plan.

Every three months or so, "the next big thing" launches and I get a flood of emails and phone calls from the poor folks who just don't get it yet; those who sincerely wonder why in the world I won't jump in on the ground floor with them.

My reason is simple...

The only way you'll make it in this industry is to become a leader with a following, but signing an application three days after a company opens its doors does not qualify you as one.

Okay, let me get off my soapbox and tell you about a conversation I had a few years ago.

I was talking with a pastor who wanted to start a home business. He had looked at my company, but his wife decided she liked another product better.

"Okay great," I said. "I'm glad to hear that you found something, John, but let me ask you a quick question. How are you going to build your business?"

John: "What do you mean?"

"Well, your product, company, and compensation plan are meaningless until you find a way to acquire your customers and business builders, right? The money is not in the product. It is in your ability to MOVE (market) that product. How are you going to do that?"

John: "Ummmm, not sure."

Exactly.

Understand that this business is all about the marketing!

- When you do this business right, you don't have to "sell."
- When you do this business right, you don't have to ask people to join your business… They ask you!
- When you do this business right, you don't have to post "work at home" flyers on car windows.
- When you do this business right, people PAY YOU to prospect them.
- When you do this business right, you and your team members make cash quickly, even from the people who DON'T join your organization.

The problem is that 99 percent of network marketers don't do it right because they don't know how to market.

Making huge lists and cold calling? No, thanks. I'd rather be fishing, so I became a voracious student of marketing because I'd rather have my system selling my product, filling my list, and bringing people to me 24/7, *all on my prospect's dime.*

Sound good to you? Thought so!

The marketing strategies and business model I'm about to share with you have made me over $50 million in the past 10 years.

It doesn't matter what you're selling, what kind of business you're building, or what industry that business is in.

I've used this exact same process to build the largest residual income check in a network marketing business. I've used it to build *Magnetic Sponsoring* into a $25 million publishing company, and I've used it to build The Elevation Group (EVG) into a $25 million plus financial education company.

We're going to start with the basics, and over the next few chapters, I'm going to teach you how to implement this exact same model in your business.

Let's get started…

Have you ever wondered why so many people struggle in this industry?

It took me a few years to figure it out, but it finally dawned on me…

Network Marketing is an industry of marketing and promotion, pursued by people who have no idea how to market or promote.

How's that for a dose of reality?

As a network marketer, you only have one job: Sell the company's products and opportunity.

The parent company does everything else for you.

They manufacture and warehouse the product. They manage the employees. They provide fulfillment, customer service, and tend to all of the accounting and legal matters.

You and the other distributors are their marketing arm, and you have one single task: Sell.

The fact that you don't have to do any of the other business management tasks is one of the primary advantages of pursing an MLM business.

But if you don't know how to market or promote effectively, you're basically screwed.

I could dump two tons of the greatest new Super Vitamin 2000 on your driveway, but unless you know how to market it to the right people, you won't make a dime. The money is not in the product. It's in knowing how to market the product.

To make matters worse, the business opportunity you're selling in network marketing is not what it seems.

It's completely counter-intuitive, but it turns out that your products and services are not really your true products. Here's what I mean...

Most networkers are either selling their business opportunity or selling their company's product.

I don't sell either one.

Instead, I sell a system to distributors. And that system effectively creates product customers.

Let me share an example with you that will help you understand what I mean. We'll use a little company named McDonald's.

When Ray Kroc founded McDonald's, he didn't care about the food or its quality. That's not why people eat there. People eat at McDonald's for the *predictable* experience, speed, and prices. What Ray perfected and SOLD to franchise owners was a *system* for consistently turning beef into cash.

After all, investors don't buy a franchise because they have some mission in life to serve tasty food. They're buying the business to make money, and Ray had perfected the system better than anyone else.

So, Ray sold a "money making restaurant system in a box" to franchisers, and the system cranked out the retail product to the customers.

Today, McDonald's is a billion-dollar franchise run by high school kids.

The only three jobs their employees have are the following:

1. Provide customer service.
2. Cook the food.
3. Train the new employees to provide customer service and cook the food.

That's it.

The system does the rest. The employees push the buttons that turn on the fryers, microwaves, and cash registers.

They simply push the "go buttons," and that is why McDonald's has succeeded. This level of duplication created a completely predictable experience for the customers, *which is McDonald's real product.* It's not their food. It's the predictable nature of their food, service, and atmosphere.

Your network marketing business should be no different.

It's a paramount concept that you need to understand from the get-go.

So how do you define a "system?"

Well, boiled down to its most basic element, a system is nothing more than a standardized set of tools and instructions.

Your system can be anything as long as there are a common set of tools and instructions.

Our job is to:

1. Market a system to distributors, which then retails the company products.
2. Teach them leadership and marketing skills to help our new distributors become "Alphas." This will allow them to effectively sell more franchises to future franchise buyers (distributors).

One of the most important lessons you can take away from this book is understanding what you're actually selling to your customers.

It's the foundation your marketing expertise will be built upon, so I'd like to share a pearl of wisdom that literally changed my life, and it's one of the most talked about parts of this book...

Read this as many times as you need to:

> "Nobody who bought a drill actually wanted a drill. They wanted a hole. Therefore, if you want to sell drills, you should advertise information about making holes—NOT information about drills!"
>
> —PERRY MARSHALL

This insight changed the way I looked at selling and marketing forever, because it's the moment I realized that people didn't buy our products because they wanted our products.

They purchased our products because they wanted the end results they would provide.

You did not buy *Magnetic Sponsoring* because you wanted a book. You bought *Magnetic Sponsoring* because you wanted to learn how to end the pain of what comes from a lack of money, or to enjoy the benefits and freedom that come with making more of it.

Last year, I purchased a year's supply of emergency food. I didn't make that purchase because I wanted "food." I really purchased peace of mind.

I didn't buy an Aston Martin with 500 HP because I needed transportation. I purchased a unique experience that only a vehicle like that can provide.

Website designers aren't selling websites. They are selling the convenience of not having to learn HTML.

Photographers aren't selling photographs, they are selling the ability to remember and conjure a feeling.

Do you really think you're selling vitamins and weight-loss products? Or are you really selling better health and more self-confidence?

So, now that you know what you're actually selling, let's talk about the actual purpose of marketing.

When some people think of "marketing" or "selling," they associate this process with manipulation and "tricking" people into buying something.

Nothing could be further from the truth.

Real, effective, long-term marketing practices are based on one thing...

Creating trust.

Specifically, marketing is the process of turning strangers into friends, friends into first-time customers, and first-time customers into life-long customers.

Think of marketing as dating.

Before you can ask for someone's hand in marriage, you have to take the time to build trust and demonstrate value.

One of the biggest reasons networks fail is because they try to force their prospect to join the business on their terms and timetable.

You want Suzy to sign up and join your team today.

Well for any number of reasons, there's a very good chance that Suzy might not be ready to join just yet.

But it doesn't mean she might not join next week or next month.

When Suzy says "no" or "not now," the amateur distributor who's sponsoring two or three distributors per month will say, "Some will, some won't, so what. Next."

The Alpha Networker who's making seven figures and sponsoring two to three distributors *per day* will say, "No problem."

The difference between the two is simple... The professional has a marketing pipeline in place that will continuously build trust and rapport with Suzy for weeks and months automatically, until she is ready to say yes. The amateur has long forgotten about Suzy, and is still dialing for dollars.

My first "real job" out of college was recruiting surgeons in Dallas for hospitals around the country. It was nowhere near as nice as it might sound.

A typical day was spent making 200 to 300 cold calls to doctors' offices trying to get through the front desk to the doctor. Out of those dials, I might reach 10 doctors a day.

Out of those 10, three of them might be interested in our services and request more information. So I might find 90 real prospects per month that have entered my "pipeline."

I'd made contact with them. I'd gathered their mailing information, phone number, and email address, and I'd sent them further information about our services.

But the next step is the key to success in sales — **constant contact over time**.

Why?

Once again, it's all about timing. Not your timing or when you want to make a sale, but when they want to buy.

Every month, I would add 90 new doctors to my pipeline, and at least twice every month, I would contact each of them either by phone, email, or mail.

The size of my prospect pipeline continued to grow month after month:

MONTH 1:	90 doctors
MONTH 2:	180
MONTH 3:	270
MONTH 4:	360
MONTH 5:	450
MONTH 6:	540
MONTH 12:	1,080

The interesting part is that most of the recruiters in my position didn't recruit their first doctor for three to six months, but once they had about 300 to 600 prospects in their pipeline, they would start recruiting three to eight doctors per month or more.

This is possible because we were staying in constant contact with our prospects and keeping track of when the timing was right for them; even if it happened to be a year down the road, we would be the first people they called or the first ad they responded to.

When you build up a pipeline with hundreds or thousands of contacts over time, the timing for someone is going to be right **every single day!**

And that, my friends, is why you always hear that "the fortune is in the follow-up."

Without a pipeline to create ongoing contact, there is no relationship built up over time, which means you're limited to the small number of people who are ready and willing to say "yes" today. This is why so many people think sponsoring is "hard," when in fact it's really easy if you have the patience and foresight to do it right.

Thanks to technology, like an email autoresponder, this entire follow-up process can be completely automated.

I'll teach you how to set up your pipeline in just a few minutes, but first I want you to understand how important and powerful this strategy really is. In fact, it's so powerful that this pipeline will eventually become your entire business…

The simple truth of the matter is that once you start to implement this strategy, you're no longer building a network marketing business.

You're building a distribution channel.

Starbucks (SB) has 23,187 locations in 61 different countries as of the time of this writing.

Those stores represent SB's distribution channel.

If they want to sell more coffee, they must expand their channel by opening more stores.

The miracle of building a business in the Internet age is that it allows a single person from their home computer to build a massive, global, virtual distribution channel.

Television is a distribution channel.

Radio is a distribution channel.

Facebook is a distribution channel.

These are the mediums in which marketing messages flow and goods are sold to a participating audience.

My goal as a business owner is to build an ever-expanding distribution channel.

In the case of *Magnetic Sponsoring* and EVG, that channel is in the form of our email newsletter lists.

Magnetic Sponsoring has about 200,000 active readers and EVG has about 400,000 readers.

Imagine how many stores I'd have to open in any given industry to get access to 600,000 interested people.

It would cost millions of dollars in infrastructure.

Thanks to the Internet, our messages and products are put directly in front of our readers, right in their homes or their cellphones, for as little as $20 per month.

With a few clicks of a mouse, I can send an email to these lists and sell millions of dollars in goods and services.

In fact, I'll be walking you through a few examples and case studies to demonstrate exactly how we do this.

Whether that list is comprised of email readers, Facebook likes, YouTube channel subscribers, or followers on Twitter, this list is like your own private TV or radio station through which you can promote your goods and services.

At the end of the day, your business is your LIST.

More specifically, it's the quality of the relationship you have with the people on your list.

The more time, attention, and affection you give to the people on your list, the more valuable and profitable it will become.

When I launched EVG, we acquired over 8,600 paying customers and produced $3.2 million in revenue within our first seven days of business, without spending a single dime on advertising.

How was that possible?

Simple...

During the previous five years, I had built a distribution channel here at *Magnetic Sponsoring* of about 200,000 people, and a fantastic relationship with them built on trust and respect.

As a result, 8,600+ people joined EVG in the very first week.

Do not underestimate the relationship component. That is everything.

For example, one of the biggest mistakes I see new marketers making online is commonly demonstrated on Twitter.

Johnny just joined his new MLM and wants to build a following on Twitter so he can promote his opportunity to his followers.

He starts following everyone he can find because many users will automatically "follow back."

He follows 10,000 people on Twitter, and has 9,000 people automatically follow him back.

Do these 9,000 people actually know Johnny and what he does?

No.

Did they follow him out of a genuine interest in his work?

No.

Do they have any kind of relationship with him?

No.

Do they know, like, and trust him?

No.

They automatically followed him because they are also seeking to artificially boost their follower count.

At the end of the day, all of these people are kidding themselves. Their Twitter lists are nothing more than an illusion with zero actual value.

They're playing a childish game that does nothing more than artificially inflate their ego.

There is only ONE way to build a real list: Earn your reader's attention the old-fashioned way by delivering value (there's that whole PVL thing again).

Once you have a virtual distribution channel and an active relationship with the people in it, selling products or sponsoring new distributors becomes effortless and can be conducted at the click of a mouse.

CHAPTER FOUR

How to Generate Endless Leads for Free

One of the biggest challenges I faced in my early years in network marketing was a lack of money. I was waiting tables and broke.

I usually had $100 to $200 per month to put towards my business, which meant I couldn't afford to advertise. It was enough to buy a few leads, but that was about it.

It's an incredibly common problem faced by most people in the industry and, unfortunately, the very nature of a multi-level compensation plan makes it very hard to overcome.

Let's say that you buy 20 leads at $5 each, for a total cost of $100. On average, 90 percent of your leads will never join your business or buy your product.

That leaves you with two people who said yes. They each purchased $100 of your Super Vitamin 2000 juice.

While compensation plans vary, you're typically going to make just 5–15 percent on your personal sales. So, if you sell $100 worth of product, you're making $5 to $15 in commission.

For simplicity's sake, let's say your commission rate in this example is 10 percent.

$200 × 10% = $20 in commissions.

So you spent $100 on leads to make $20 for a loss of -$80.

The only way these numbers turn positive is when you recruit others and make a commission on their volume, or you stop buying leads and recruit 100 percent from your warm market.

What happens if you don't have a warm market or don't want to sell to them?

You're screwed.

But there is a solution and, in fact, it's the secret to not just making a few thousand dollars per month, but a few MILLION.

If you think it has something to do with the 90 percent of your leads who said "no" to your product and opportunity, you're correct.

The secret is to change your perspective, your mission, and your end goal.

You have two choices...

You can do what most people do and put 100 percent of your focus on building your network marketing opportunity and working with the 10 percent of your leads who joined you or became customers.

– Or –

You can do what I did and put 100 percent of your focus on serving 100 percent of your leads, whether they joined your business or not.

Just because they didn't buy your opportunity doesn't mean they won't buy another product or service from you.

This realization was a massive turning point in my career.

My mission changed from simply building a downline, to helping as many people as I could to reach their goal of financial freedom, whether they joined me or not.

Think about that for a minute.

Instantly, my potential customer pool went from that tiny 10 percent of my leads who joined my business, TO THE ENTIRE INDUSTRY.

Even if you were in another MLM company and very happy there, I could still turn you into a customer for other products or services that could help you grow your business.

As a result, it created an **entirely new business model**.

Here's an extremely simplified version before we dive into the details:

Step 1: My focus changed from selling my MLM opportunity, to building a distribution channel (or as we'll call it from this point forward, a "list").

I build my list by placing ads online offering something of value such as a free training video, in exchange for the person's email address.

Step 2: I build a relationship with the people on that list by sending valuable training and content via email. This allows those individuals to get to know me as an individual, mentor and leader with a high PVL. As a result, it builds attraction, affinity, and trust.

Step 3: I market to that list by offering products and services that will help them get what they want, whether it's my network marketing opportunity, or generic training courses on personal development, marketing, etc.

In its most simplified form, my business model can be summed up like this:

1. Build a list.
2. Build a relationship with the people on that list.
3. Market to the list.

The financial implications of this new model were revolutionary to my business and everyone else who has implemented it for one primary reason...

You no longer have to recruit someone or sell your product in order to make money.

You can make money even if they don't join you, which means you can afford to advertise, which means you can generate endless leads, which means you can sponsor more distributors.

Now, let's take a deeper look at the pieces that make up our new business model, which can also be considered a "marketing funnel."

From clicking on an advertisement to becoming a lifelong customer, the marketing funnel is the journey a prospect takes through your buying process. The purpose of a marketing funnel is to create a controlled path for the person to travel as they go from a cold prospect to an active paying customer.

The "bones" of this funnel can be applied to ANY kind of business, in ANY kind of industry.

At the end of the day, this is an outline for a marketing and sales process. The goods or services you can plug into it are completely interchangeable.

I've used this exact same process to sell everything from an MLM opportunity, to e-books, to boxes of tea, to financial education.

While most companies that don't understand marketing will put up a website and then keep their fingers crossed that people will buy from them, we craft and cater our marketing funnel experience to actively lead people to the outcome we desire, which is the purchase of a product or service.

Here is a visual image of our sales funnel, which is essentially a five-step process.

The order of your marketing pipeline is as follows: ADVERTISING » LEAD CAPTURE » "SELLACATION" » FRONT-END RETAIL » YOUR MLM/BACK END PROMOS » RESIDUALS.

Let's go through these steps to get an idea of what each one entails.

STEP 1: ADVERTISING

All marketing starts with advertising, getting your message and your offer out into the world — and as far as we're concerned, there are two types of advertising:

1. Direct Response – Advertising designed to elicit a response of some kind from the audience, whether it's to call a phone number, go to a webpage, fill out a form, or make a purchase.

By definition, any and every part of a direct response ad campaign can and should be measured, from the initial exposure to the final exchange of money. Thanks to the Internet, that is extremely easy to do.

2. Image Advertising – This is what 95 percent of all network marketing companies use (probably because they don't know any better).

Image advertising concentrates on selling the company's logo, history, story, and goals, and is not designed to elicit a specific action by the audience. Basically, it's designed to increase branding and make the audience "feel good" about the company, which is not something that can be accurately measured.

You really don't know if it's making you money from the specific advertising dollars you're spending in the end or not, which is a luxury that can only be afforded by the big guys of corporate America. Think Coke, Pepsi, Lexus, etc.

But there's one tiny problem when that kind of advertising is used in the MLM industry:

Your prospects don't really give a hoot about your product or company. As we've learned, they don't care that your company was founded 20 years ago, or that your product has a patent, or that it's debt-free.

All they care about is whether or not it will provide a solution to their problems by increasing their income, bringing them better health, saving them money on long-distance, etc., and whether or not you are someone who can help them reach those goals.

As network marketers and Internet marketers, the only kind of advertising we are interested in is direct response, because that's the kind of advertising that sells and puts money in our pockets or new reps in our downline.

STEP 2: LEAD CAPTURE

This is the single most important part of your entire marketing process!

A lead capture page is also called a landing page or gateway page.

These are all different names for the same thing—a webpage that exists for one single reason: To capture the contact information of the visitor.

It has no other purpose but to gather their contact information, turning visitors into leads. This page literally *adds people to your list* every time they type their email address into the form and hit submit. You can't build an email list without a capture page.

Now that we've added them to our list, we can continue to communicate with them, build a relationship with them, and market to them.

Your capture page is the *front door* to the rest of the process, and you're going to see examples of many of them throughout this book.

STEP 3: SELLACATION

This is a term I coined a while back and it simply refers to the concept of "selling through education." Here's a little human psychology to keep in mind as you develop your marketing skills:

- People do not like to be sold, but they DO like to buy.
- Getting people to purchase your products and services is EASY as long as it's their idea to buy it.
- It's much more effective to pull people to your product by educating them on the benefits over time, than it is to push your product on them because you want to make a sale.

In the *sellacation* process, we are doing several things:

1. We're providing value to our prospects by giving them free education whether they buy from us or not.
2. The valuable education we provide through constant communication serves to build a relationship that establishes attraction, trust, and respect. They come to see us as a person who can provide them with solutions to their problems.
3. By positioning our product, business, or service as the solution of choice within the education process, we're pulling them towards the purchase. We make it their idea to buy the next step in our pipeline, which is to purchase our front-end retail product.

STEP 4: SELLING A FRONT-END RETAIL PRODUCT

As we've discussed, one of the biggest problems you see in the

MLM industry is that reps spend more money than they make, and it happens because they aren't generating a retail income to fund their business activities.

Like it or not, retailing products is a VERY IMPORTANT part of getting a network marketing business off the ground and into profitability, but there are some challenges involved...

1. Many business builders don't want to sell things to their friends and family members. Or...
2. They run out of potential retail prospects. Everyone's warm market has a limited size unless you start producing referrals. This is an option, but in the end, it's just not possible or practical for the average, part-time network marketer to make a retail sale of their product every single day in a duplicable manner.

Nonetheless, retail income is a must-have component of any profitable business because it serves several critical purposes:

First, it's much easier to sell a $17 to $47 retail product to someone than it is to sell a product, service, or business opportunity that costs $200 to $5,000.

By marketing an inexpensive product on the front end, you give people an opportunity to take a "test-drive" of you, your products, and your services without making a massive monetary commitment.

Retailing gives you an opportunity to build trust with new customers so you can turn them into life-long customers.

This is a critical step in your business model because it's always easier and more profitable to up-sell an existing customer than it is to create a new one from scratch.

Most networkers just call their leads, who are complete strangers, and pitch them on a business opportunity. "Hey, you don't know me, but if you send me $300, we can go into business together and get rich selling these nifty vitamins."

There is no relationship in place.

It's much more effective to start small. Earn trust. Extend value. And THEN upgrade that customer into a business owner.

Another advantage of retailing a low-cost front-end product is that it gives you an opportunity to advertise and create new customers for FREE (or close to it).

The income from your retail sales is designed to do one thing:

Pay the C.T.A. (Cost to Acquire) you incurred to produce that customer. The revenues from retail sales should cover most, if not all, of the expenses you incurred to produce that sale such as the cost of the ads, marketing pieces, etc.

Let's say I spend $100 on ads for Facebook, and for $400, I end up producing 100 leads, resulting in a cost per lead of $4.00 each.

After these 100 people opt into my capture page, I present them with a video that sells a $50 e-book on how to build a home business.

A really good conversion rate would be 8 percent, which means 8 out of my 100 leads end up purchasing the e-book immediately, which puts $400 back in my pocket.

As you can see, I've just recouped my advertising costs before I've even spoken to a single person or pitched my MLM opportunity.

This means I can afford to generate as many leads as I want for FREE. I've added 100 new leads to my list, at a net cost of $0.00.

This method is called a "**funded-proposal**," where people essentially pay you to become a lead.

But it gets better...

If you call those 100 leads, 5 to 10 percent will end up joining your MLM opportunity now or at some point in the future, which means you're now making a significant profit.

I prefer to sell information products as my "retail front-end product" because you need some high profit margins in order for this "funded proposal" model to work.

Selling a $40 nutrition product that pays you $15 in retail commissions isn't going to cut it.

On the other hand, information products can typically be sold at a 50 to 100 percent profit, which is what you're looking for.

The trick is to align the topic of the information product to the wants and desires of the prospect. For a business opportunity lead, I'm going to promote a "how to" course on building a successful home business.

For a product customer with health issues, I'm going to retail a "how to" course on staying healthy naturally.

Don't worry if you don't have a product like this to retail to your leads.

You don't need to create your own because there are plenty of high quality products already available that will pay you an affiliate commission.

STEP 5: GENERATING BACK-END REVENUE

Now it's time to take advantage of our retailing efforts and extend our retail customers "back-end" offers.

We've built trust and a relationship with our retail customers. They've spent money with us and experienced our product or service, which has "over-delivered" and exceeded their expectations.

They are now raving fans of "You Inc." and the products you market, who can't wait to buy from you again because they received so much value from their first purchase.

The quality and value of your retail product is critical to making big money on the back-end.

If you over-deliver and exceed their expectations, they will become life-long customers.

If your product was mediocre or worse, they are gone forever.

Always put your best foot forward with your front-end retail efforts and strive to overwhelm people with the amount of value they received for the price.

Okay, so a few months have gone by and your list has grown to 5,000 leads.

Seven percent of them purchased your $50 e-book, producing 350 front-end customers and $17,500 in revenue. You've taken that

$17,500 and used it to cover your advertising costs.

Which means that your profit at this moment is $0.00.

Now it's time to market back-end products to your 350 front-end customers.

These are products or services that are related to the retail product, but they offer more — more information, more abilities, more options, etc. — this means they will also cost more.

A typical back-end product will cost $100 to $2,000+, and this is where your *profit* is made.

You can upgrade them to a business builder, increase their auto-ship order, or up-sell them a high-end information product or course.

For over 10 years, I used this very book, *Magnetic Sponsoring*, as my front-end retail product to build my businesses. People loved it and they wanted to learn more, so I created Black Belt Recruiting, a course on how to talk to your prospects on the phone, and MLM Traffic Formula, which was an extremely detailed online marketing course. I sold them for $97 and $297.

At EVG, we have an entrepreneurial course called "Elevation Income" that we offer our front-end customers for $2,000.

Because our 350 customers have come to know us, like our work, and trust us, they are much more likely to buy our back-end offers.

Instead of a 7 percent conversion rate, you can expect to see a 20 to 30 percent conversion rate.

So let's say that you offer them an advanced course on how to generate leads online for $1,000, and 25 percent of your 350 customers buy.

Congratulations. *You've just made $87,500* and the vast majority of that is profit.

Here's the crazy part… You haven't even mentioned or promoted your MLM opportunity yet. You haven't even called a single lead.

And this brings us to the final piece of our revenue model, "Residual Income." This is where your primary MLM opportunity comes into play.

Residual income is meant to be built up and acquired over a long period of time. Your residual money is "extra" money. It's 100 percent profit and it should not be used to fund your business-building process.

When building a list of networkers that you can build relationships with over time, it is essential that you market and offer generic information of value. You can then begin marketing your primary MLM to these contacts over time or give them the opportunity to opt-in to information about your company within your newsletters and communications.

You want them to buy into "YOU" before you approach them about a business, and it gives you the opportunity to monetize the people on your list through product offers or affiliate promotions, whether they join you or not.

This is a LONG-TERM pipeline strategy.

Now, here's the big question that I get asked all of the time: "Mike, if I'm advertising generic information targeted to other network marketers, when do I bring up my opportunity?"

Here's the interesting part... You can bring it up if you want, or you can be very subtle about it.

Most people will simply call you or email you and ask, especially if you're sending them emails with valuable training information or successful case studies about your downline members.

With that in mind, here's some advice:

You don't want to convince someone that they need to come join you and your opportunity because "it's better" in one way or another. Someone who proactively pursues and attempts to cross-recruit someone else who's in another business is a sleazy Beta with low integrity. Beside the fact that they're poaching and hurting someone else's business, it's not going to work out well anyway...

The person being recruited will likely do very little and quit within 90 days. Why? Because they joined for the wrong reasons. They were persuaded and maybe even pressured by the recruiter who took advantage of their lack of belief in themselves or their current business.

Can you recruit other network marketers? YES. In fact that's all I do, and we'll talk about that in detail in a later chapter.

But I never, ever, actively recruited and persuaded another net-worker away from their existing business.

I marketed my message online. If it resonated with them, but were in another business, they had to pursue what they really wanted. If they wanted to join me, they were welcome to, but it had to be their idea.

Whatever they wanted to do was 100% their decision. A decision that was made without pressure or persuasion, which means that if they joined my team, they showed up for the right reasons, with a clear head, and ready to rock.

This buy-in process happens *when the time is right for them.* You must understand this, accept it, and build your marketing plan around it.

Because this is a long-term process, you need to make sure that your prospects are willing to continue accepting and reading your communications to them.

The only way they will do that is if you continually offer them value through education. Your prospects will read your emails and letters only if you have earned that right by delivering valuable content they find useful in their business endeavors.

But that still leaves us with the original question: How do we finally get our opportunity in front of them?

Here are two ways:

1. Within your communications, give them the ability to opt-in to information about your company in a passive manner. For example, you could include a link to a capture page for your primary opportunity in your signature line at the end of your email, along with a compelling teaser statement. Remember, this voluntary opt-in to a passive or subtle information source for your opportunity is critical because it needs to be their idea. They need to pursue the information.
2. Weave your opportunity in your educational emails through examples or stories. Did you see a downline member accomplish something really great? How did they do it? Weave their story into a training message so the email still holds real value,

but gets your company name into the air in an unobtrusive way. This method positions you as a team leader giving applause to an active downline member. It is a success story/testimonial that involves you and your team, providing social proof that people win when they work with you.

CHAPTER FIVE

How to Find the Best Prospects for Your Business

Alright, so we've determined that the best way to succeed in this industry is to use marketing effectively, and one of the most important steps of effective marketing is to know who your target audience is and how to find them.

Let's say that you've just inherited $20,000 from your Uncle Bob who just died in a goat wrangling accident, and you've decided you're going to blow up your business "big time" by plowing all of it into an advertising campaign.

Clearly, everyone who learns about your opportunity is going to join. It's the biggest ground-floor opportunity you've ever seen in your life. As far as you're concerned, you'd have to be an idiot to pass this by.

You want your ad to be seen by as many successful business people as possible, so you decide to spend all $20,000 on a full-page ad in the *Wall Street Journal*.

The paper with your ad hits the streets and you can hardly contain yourself because this is your big moment. Your idea is genius, and it's about to make you the number one earner in your company.

But it doesn't. In fact, you get a whopping eight phone calls over the next few days, and not a single person joined your downline.

Why? What went wrong?

One of the biggest secrets to successful advertising is to know who your target market is, and only advertise to the people in it.

No matter what kind of business you're building or industry you're in, your target market is always the same... *It's people who have purchased a similar product or service before, or people who are actively searching out your product or service today.* That's it.

In our case, the only people who are in our primary target market are those who have been in network marketing before, who are in it today, or who are actively buying information about it (like this book).

In short, we want to market to people who have already purchased a home-based business at one time or another — other networkers.

Why?

- Network marketers already **believe** in the business model.
- Network marketers have already **spent money** on the industry.
- Network marketers **want** to succeed.
- Network marketers are **willing and eager** to purchase anything that will help them succeed.

The difference is like placing ads in every major newspaper looking for ANYONE "who would like to play professional baseball" and trying to train them to become a pro, or going directly to people who already play professional baseball and sponsoring them onto your team.

When it comes to recruiting new distributors, only invest in ads that target network marketers. Yes, you can go after talented and successful people in your warm market, and I suggest you do, but that should happen as an "add-on." In other words, go after your warm market contacts when the opportunity arises, but do not make them your sole focus.

It is an uphill battle you will not win.

Opportunity leads are simply "opportunity seekers." They are tire-kickers.

Network marketers are **"opportunity buyers,"** and we sell a business opportunity!

I sell to people who *already buy* what I have to offer. I only enroll people who want to be enrolled! Crazy, aren't I!?

Sending a CD or your web address to Uncle Bob, the plumber, and your softball buddy, Tim, is a little like this: Let's say you're an award-winning chef who's come up with a steak dish that is considered pure perfection — the cow raised on the purest feed in the world and prepared by your skilled hands... Flavor-worthy of a $100 price tag for just eight heavenly ounces.

But, it just so happens that you work at a vegetarian restaurant. As you might guess, despite all of its merits and applause, *you couldn't give that perfect dish away for free to the diners at a vegetarian restaurant.*

They're not in your target market.

On the other hand, you could walk next door to The Steak Baron's Inn, and within 10 minutes, the dish would be sold out. They might even dedicate a full page of the menu just to your example of beef perfection — and you'd make some serious cash!

If you want to make your life easy, make a lot of cash, and have a lot of fun doing it, stay within your target market (network marketers), and those looking to buy into network marketing!

WHERE TO FIND CONTACT INFORMATION
FOR NETWORK MARKETERS

A few years ago, the most common answer was to use genealogy lists. Genealogies are a heavy hitter's downline report of those who have left the industry or the distributor database from a company who has gone out of business.

The problem with genealogies is that an average of 40 percent of the information is outdated and incorrect. The list may have been released yesterday, but some of the reps on it may have joined the company 10 years ago!

This renders a list like this useless for any kind of direct mail campaign, and emailing them would be considered spam and illegal. The only method available is cold calling the list, which is extremely inefficient (I know from experience).

Therefore, the best way to get in touch with other networkers is to:

Advertise.

Placing ads in industry journals, work at home magazines, and on Google works great if you have an effective ad and practice *Magnetic Sponsoring* by promoting a generic solution. Simply advertising and soliciting for leads for your opportunity will suck your bank account dry because other networkers don't care about your business, as they probably have one already.

Advertise your MLM and you will lose money! No one cares about your MLM! They are already in one!

"So what the heck do I advertise, Mike?"

"Why would I advertise for other networkers if they won't join me anyway?"

Great question!

The key to effective marketing (and *Magnetic Sponsoring*) is to promote and *sell* a generic *solution and system*, *instead* of your business opportunity on the front end.

You see, most people would rather learn how to do something, than actually do it.

For example... Of the following, which ad would you respond to?

"Join my company XYZ and make six figures in three months!"

Or:

"Revealed: How I built a million dollar business from my home on a shoe-string budget. Step-by-step instructions."

If you're like most people, you would choose ad number two. It holds a higher perceived value and it's generic.

It doesn't exclude anyone. It's helpful and hopeful, so it will get a much higher response. Not to mention that you already went down road number one. It sucked. You lost money. You lost credibility. It was painful, and you are looking for a way to reach the prize without any pain.

So, you're going to advertise two things:

1. Your Alpha self because people don't join business opportunities; they join other people (Alpha leaders, specifically).
2. Your marketing system. Just like Ray Kroc, you're going to sell a marketing system to distributors. That system should sell your company's products.

What does every single networker need help doing? Recruiting customers and business builders, right? Right. So I market a solution to that problem in the form of a complete system that shows them how they will build their business.

If you can show someone how they're going to build their business with a proven system, and they can see themselves doing it successfully, they will join you. Period.

Finally, I bring my opportunity into focus as a solution to other problems faced in this industry. After I market the How, I market the Who, What, When, Where, and Why of my company.

This marketing order is the exact *opposite* of the average networker who leads with: Who, What, When, Where, and Why of his company, and then he might get to the How after a person joins the team.

CHAPTER SIX

How to Create a Marketing Machine That Recruits for You

We've seen the five components of this business model. We've discovered the difference between selling products and selling solutions. Now I'm going to show you how to take this strategy into the market place.

We have three goals for our marketing pipeline:

1. We want it to communicate to our prospects automatically over an extended period of time. This is most often and effectively done by creating an email newsletter series, which is sent to your prospects on a pre-determined schedule.

An autoresponder service costs approximately $20 per month. You can check out the ones I recommend, along with other resources at www.MagneticSponsoring.com/bonus.

Remember, in order to make a significant income (more than a doctor), you must be able to impact a significant number of people. This small $20 service is the tool that will provide you with the ability to leverage your message.

These emails should build trust and rapport, positioning you as a leader. The best way to do that is to teach your readers something of value that will help them reach their goal of financial freedom.

You want to make it easy for your readers to contact you by placing your contact information in every email. Many of your prospects will reach out, and once you get the prospect to call you first — instead of hunting him or her down — suddenly you're in charge. You've successfully positioned yourself as an expert resource instead of a peddler, and that's when sponsoring becomes effortless.

2. We want this series of emails to promote and sell a front-end product for us automatically. It should be priced from $17 to $47, and they should be able to order this product online 24 hours per day without contacting you personally. This could be a bottle of your nutrition product, a training e-book, or an affiliate product you make a commission on.

3. We want to promote back-end products and services to our pipeline via email, such as your network marketing products or opportunity, advanced training courses, or affiliate products and services.

While the majority of communication with the people on your list is done via email, you can supplement your communication channels by instructing them to follow you on Facebook, Twitter, YouTube, or whatever social media channels you prefer. With that in mind, remember that the most effective channel still is, and will continue to be, email.

How do you actually create an email newsletter? Great question.

To start a "Magnetic" newsletter, you need four things:

- A website where prospects can opt-in or request your newsletter in exchange for something of value. As mentioned earlier, this is commonly referred to as a capture page or landing page.
- An advertising campaign to send traffic to your capture page.
- A newsletter that offers truly valuable information to your subscribers.
- An email autoresponder service that will deliver your newsletter.

By now, you know that the key to success is to provide your prospects with high quality information that will help them get what **they want, without directly pitching them on your opportunity**. They must learn to like you and trust you before they will follow you.

Don't just throw some sloppy newsletter together in two days. Spend as much time as it takes to "wow" them. *Over-deliver.* The quality of your information will have a direct impact on the effectiveness of your overall strategy. Providing poor information will repel more people than it will attract.

You might be saying, "Well, Mike, that sounds great and all, but I wouldn't know what to write! I've yet to succeed myself, so how can I teach someone how to do it better!?"

Well, I'm happy to tell you that *you* don't have to (you just have to know someone who can!)

A tactic used by both experts and non-experts is the interview.

You can be completely clueless on a topic or brand new to this industry, but accomplish your goal by interviewing an expert.

Top Internet marketers make millions of dollars selling products they never produced themselves. They simply interview an expert in their field, package it, and then sell it!

You can do the same thing:

- Who in your upline is the top recruiter? Go interview him/her.
- Who in your upline is the top trainer? Go interview him/her.
- Who specializes in home business tax strategies?
- Who knows how to write persuasive emails and sales pieces?
- Who is a lead generation expert?
- Who is off to a huge start in your company? How did they do it?
- Who is your favorite MLM guru and why?
- Etc.

This is exactly how I built EVG into a $25 million business in 36 months.

I am not an investing guru. I didn't know the first thing about investing when I started the company. Instead, I simply produced video interviews with people who ARE some of the best investors on the planet, and those videos became our product.

We used this exact same marketing pipeline process to sell access to these interviews for $97 per month. In the first three years, over 50,000 people joined as paid customers.

You do NOT need to be the expert. You do NOT have to have a previous track record of success.

Alright, off the soapbox and moving on...

I'd recommend that you write at least seven emails before you start promoting your newsletter and acquiring readers. Set up your autoresponder for one email to go out each day for seven days.

This is what I did when I started *Magnetic Sponsoring*. I created a free "7-Day Boot Camp" email series people could request.

Each day for seven days, they would get an email from me with a link to a free *Magnetic Sponsoring* training video.

Every week, I'd set aside a few hours to write new emails, and add them to my autoresponder series.

Typically, I'd try to send my readers around three emails per week.

As time went by and more emails were added to my autoresponder, I soon had an entire year's worth of content being sent out to my subscribers automatically.

Here are some completely fictitious examples of email headlines and topics you could write about:

- The secret to selecting a product that sells faster than a turkey on Thanksgiving
- The top five traits every small business owner must have to succeed
- The top five mistakes that will cost you thousands
- Why the IRS paid me $1,789.00 this year just to take my vitamins
- How to effectively market a product without bugging your friends and family members
- How to "recruit" new business partners even if you hate to sell
- Why our turn-key franchise system makes building a home business easier than baking a cake
- Upline leaders finally share their secret tricks of the trade

- How to make $500/month within 60 days
- From waiting tables to $100,000 in 14 months — How she did it!
- How you train your organization
- The best and worst traits of five compensation plans revealed
- Check out these success stories

As you can see, this is useful and valuable information that someone would truly like to receive.

These emails and articles don't have to be long; they just need to give quality content and benefits. I like to put them in the form of a story or interview because that brings in the two elements you need:

1. Value – Create content that educates so they will read it, and include benefits so they will want it.
2. A personal story – Bring emotion into the message. People don't remember facts and figures; they remember stories! They make decisions based on emotion, and then justify those decisions with logic! Give them both!

Drip, drip, drip… Your newsletter arrives in their mailbox like a gift of knowledge from you. As the weeks and months go by, they also see consistency. Unlike the other people who pitch them on a new deal every six weeks, they see that you are committed to your company and your product. They see you are committed to helping your team and that you are the real deal.

Before you know it, the recipients of your newsletter will start calling you with questions or asking for your advice. This is your chance to start building a relationship with them.

They will come to like you, trust you, and join you, because you are the only person who has been truly helping them each week without trying to cram an opportunity down their throat.

Just sign each of your newsletters with your name, number, and website URL, which is preferably the address to your business-building system site (*Networkers respond to systems more than they do to a company or product*).

The simple fact that you're writing and sending a newsletter means that you're an Alpha, because they are following you by simply "following" your newsletter. Because they see you as an Alpha, they will naturally be attracted to you (remember: attraction is NOT a choice; it's a response).

The best way to learn a new skill or marketing technique is to see it and experience it for yourself.

If you'd like to model my newsletters, simply head to www.Mike-Dillard.com and subscribe.

CHAPTER SEVEN

The Million-Dollar Skill and How to Get It

Earlier in the introduction, I told you that I went from waiting tables to making seven figures once I stopped chasing opportunities and started increasing my value to the world by acquiring a new skill... But I didn't tell you which skill I acquired.

Well, that time has come.

As you've learned, network marketing is an industry of marketing and promotion pursued by people who usually have no idea how to market or promote.

Because they come into a marketing business "unskilled," they are told (and sold) on the idea that all they'll need to do is find three buddies who will find three buddies, and then they'll become rich.

This simplistic approach is justified in the name of duplication.

Let me ask you this:

Do you know a single "unskilled" person in your company that's making $100,000 to $1 million per year? Or are the people who are making that kind of money ridiculously skilled at this business and treat it with an incredible amount of attention and professionalism?

If you want to go out and acquire a few retail product customers so you can get your product for free each month, then by all means hand out some samples, videos, or business cards and you'll hit your goal.

If you want to make REAL money, you must master the skills of this industry: marketing and promotion.

I define marketing as, "the ability to communicate a message persuasively." And the skill required to communicate persuasively is **copywriting**.

As defined by Wikipedia, "Copywriting is writing copy for the purpose of advertising or marketing. The copy is meant to persuade someone to buy a product, or influence their beliefs."

I like to think of it as "salesmanship in print."

Years ago, I discovered that you can craft an entire sales presentation in the form of a written letter, which would do all of the telling and selling for you. This letter can be posted on a webpage or used as a script for a video, at which point it becomes a tireless sales robot.

It tells the story of your product, talks about its benefits, answers any objections, provides testimonials, and ultimately takes the customer's credit card and processes their order.

While I was limited to making 5–10 sales presentations per day over the phone or in person, this sales robot could give thousands of presentations per day to people all over the world, and it would do it perfectly every single time.

All hands-free, automatically, 24 hours per day, 7 days per week.

Who do you think will do better?

The polished sales master who is so good he could make 10 presentations per day and close 90 percent of them, or the kid like me who could make 1,000 presentations per day and close 10 percent?

The master would make nine sales per day working his tail off.

I would make 100 sales while sitting by the pool. I win.

And I win because that automated sales presentation gave me the one thing the master did not have... Leverage.

This is how I went from waiting tables to making seven figures within 18 months, and how I helped change an industry which had never heard of direct response marketing before.

As a new business owner, nothing is more important than generating revenue by selling your product or service, and if you want to sell, you need to learn how to write a sales presentation.

There is no other skill you could dedicate a few months of your life to that will have such a massive impact on your financial prosperity. To learn copywriting is to learn how to turn your thoughts into money.

It is the gateway skill to lifelong wealth. Once you own it, no one can take it away from you. Master it and you will never have to worry about money again.

Now, why is it so important to a network marketing business?

Because your marketing campaigns will only be as effective as its weakest link.

Let me explain...

Let's say you spend $1,000 to place an ad on Facebook for a few days. If your headline in that ad isn't written with skill, you won't get very many people to click on it.

If your capture page is weak, you won't convert your visitors into leads.

If your sales letter is weak, you won't make money, sell your products, or sponsor distributors, and that $1,000 just went down the drain.

Everything, no matter how small or seemingly insignificant, *must be sold.*

- You have to sell your prospects on why they should give you their attention and look at your ad.
- You have to sell your prospects on reading what you have to say in the ad, and then why they should continue to read further.
- Then you have to give them reasons why they should buy. You have to give them reasons why their fears should be set aside, and why their deepest desires will be fulfilled.
- You'll have to sell your prospects on your products' credibility and that your products will provide the benefits that you've promised.
- You'll have to sell them on the value of your offer and that the price you're asking is peanuts compared to what they'll get in return.
- You'll have to sell them on the fact that there is no downside

to buying from you and accepting your generous offer.
- And finally, you'll have to sell your prospects on taking action NOW. That hesitating in any way will be harmful to his/her ultimate goal of attaining pleasure or avoiding pain.

The subject line in your email must sell the person on opening it. The first sentences of your email must sell the person on continuing to read it. The body of that email must sell them on taking a particular action.

The training site for your distributors must sell them on getting started and taking action. It must sell them on following the system and on the efficacy of the company's products.

You must adopt the mental position that every single person you send a communication to is a lazy couch potato who must be truly inspired and motivated through the promise that if they pay attention to your offer, they will benefit in a substantial way.

Take this same position with your downline. Why should they buy your company's replicated site? Attend your training calls? Come to the national events?

Don't just give them a laundry list of things they need to do in order to get their business started. *Sell them on how they will benefit* by doing those things.

Let me ask you a question…

What's the difference between a million-dollar idea or opportunity and $1 million in your bank account?

The answer: Million-dollar execution.

It's not the opportunity that's worth a million bucks, it's your ability to effectively execute that opportunity.

If this is a business of marketing and promotion, then copywriting is the marketing skill required to execute your business-building tasks successfully.

The fastest way to get you to a "functional" level when it comes to copywriting is to start by studying the work of other successful copywriters.

Have you ever noticed what happens after you start spending a lot of time with a particular person? You start talking like them. You start using similar words. It's the same situation here.

By reading successful sales letters and advertisements each day, you start to adopt the same language and speech patterns of the copywriters who wrote them.

You start to use the same words and phrases. You start to get a feel for the flow of a sales letter. After time, you start writing and speaking like them as well. You can literally absorb the skill of copywriting at a subconscious level by exposing yourself to enough of it.

If you want to supercharge this learning strategy, write out these sales letters word-for-word by hand for one hour each night. This is how I started, and eventually, I had read and copied so many sales letters by hand that I just started talking and typing with the same style and language.

It's like playing the guitar for the first time. The easiest way to learn is to simply mimic the placement of your fingers on the strings. You don't need to go out and learn how to read music or memorize scales in order to play in the beginning.

This modeling process will get you to a functional place within 3–6 months, but you'll never truly master this skill until you understand the second piece to the puzzle, which is the reason why sales copy works in the first place…

Human psychology.

Copywriting is the skill and ability to persuade people to take a particular action or adopt a particular viewpoint or opinion. In any situation, the ideas, concepts, and beliefs of the person with the strongest reality will be adopted by the other.

Have you ever heard that saying, "Sales are a transfer of belief from one person to another"? Well, that's what that means.

When a sale is made, it means that your belief, or your reality, was stronger than the other person's, and so they adopted it. They bought what you were selling because they bought into your reality.

So how do you translate your beliefs to thousands or even millions of people? There's actually a scientific formula to the process I'm going to teach you in just a minute.

The psychology behind this formula is based on the fact that people buy based on emotions, and then justify making those purchases with logic. Therefore, as a sales person, we must learn how to instill certain emotional states and trigger desires in our prospects if we want them to respond to our offer.

For example, years ago I passed by a Mercedes convertible on the road that I had never seen before. Instantly, I had to have one. It has always been a deep emotional desire of mine to buy an over-the-top sports car when I "made it" — one of those things on my "dream list."

Obviously, I made a detour to the dealership. As I began shopping, I quickly became frustrated because there wasn't a single car that had the options I wanted inside the entire US, and it was going to take three months for a custom version of it to arrive from overseas.

So what happened?

I ended up looking at one that had everything I wanted with the exception of a smaller engine… And it could be at my doorstep in two weeks.

The emotional side of me instantly said "yes." I justified that decision based on the "logic" that a smaller engine would be a safer, less-expensive choice even though it wasn't what I really wanted.

Now, let's pretend that I work in the marketing department at Mercedes, and my assignment is to write an advertisement selling the smaller, 300HP engine instead of the 500HP AMG version.

Some of my copy might go like this:

"Not only will you beam with pride and personal satisfaction as you confidently drive your new Mercedes Benz each morning to the office, but the incredibly fuel-efficient aluminum V6 and 7-speed transmission will also save you money at the pump every time you take a spin."

As you can see, I start with the desired emotion and then give the reader the ability to justify their decision to buy with the logical feature to save money.

When we're writing sales copy, we're influencing people to take a specific action (like joining your opportunity), by stirring up their emotions and then offering a solution.

While the topic of copywriting is as deep as the ocean is blue, I'd like to give you a very basic, but very effective guide to writing an effective sales piece. This formula can be used to recruit distributors, sell your product, or anything for that matter…

My Step-By-Step Copywriting Guide

STEP 1: IDENTIFY YOUR TARGET AUDIENCE

The key to effective advertising and marketing is to make sure you identify your target audience as soon as possible. This is usually done in the very first sentence of text, (commonly referred to as a "pre-headline"), such as:

"Attention network marketers…" or "Looking to start a home business?"

If the person looking at your website or your ad can't tell if it's relevant to them or not within three seconds, they will leave.

The single biggest factor that has contributed to the success of my marketing pieces is that I know the people in my market (networkers) better than they know themselves.

I know their pains, fears, desires, and problems intimately because I've personally experienced each of them during my career.

I know a networker has started to figure out that the company or the product isn't really the issue by their third opportunity.

I know most of them are deathly afraid of being judged by friends and family members.

I know the ones with an incredible conviction and belief in their opportunity are completely baffled as to why their doctor, boss, CPA, or co-workers continue to ignore their pleas to look at their opportunity.

I know that most don't have the money to buy leads nor the knowledge to generate their own…

…And the list could go on and on.

If you're selling a health product for arthritis but don't have arthritis yourself, you're going to have a hard time writing about a solution for it effectively because there's no way you can truly understand how it feels to live with that disease. This means there's no way you can truly describe the pain, discomfort, and everyday hassles it creates.

If that's the case, then contact and interview someone who DOES have arthritis or who is a part of your target market. Get in their head. Spend a day in their shoes.

STEP 2: IDENTIFY THEIR MOST URGENT PAIN OR DESIRE

After you identify your target audience, you want to acknowledge their most urgent pain, problem, or desire. This is usually done in the headline. Knowing your target audience's core desire is critical for this step.

What do most network marketers want most?

They want to make money, sponsor more distributors, and build a downline.

What are their biggest problems or fears?

They have no idea how to generate leads or advertise. Many of them are scared to approach their friends and family members or talk to their leads on the phone. They're afraid they'll run out of money, be judged by others, etc.

STEP 3: OFFER A UNIQUE SOLUTION

Once you've identified your target audience and their biggest source of pain, it's time to offer your unique solution to that pain. This is best done through a story of how you had the same pain and then found the solution that solved it.

There's no need to come off as a used car salesman here. People respond to my marketing pieces because I don't use hype.

Hype is the sign of an unskilled marketer's desperate last attempt to make a sale. Talk to your prospects as if you're talking to a friend. Be real. Don't be afraid to be yourself.

If you've recently had good or bad experiences in life, share them. Were you rejected? Did you lose your distributorship? Did you take an amazing trip that's been on your bucket list? Talk about it! Turn these trials and triumphs into lessons learned for your readers. It's this kind of personal rapport that builds trust.

I can't tell you how many times I've met *Magnetic Sponsoring* students at industry events, and despite the fact that we've never met before, they feel like they know me because I share the details of my life with them.

Facts tell, stories sell.

STEP 4: PROVIDE UNQUESTIONABLE PROOF

Did you learn how to market online and generate your own leads? Show some screenshots and prove it!

Did you find a weight loss supplement that helped you lose 20 pounds? Show those before and after pictures!

Does your product have scientific studies to back it up? Link to them.

Always, always, always, use *specific* numbers in your ads whenever you can.

For example, here's a headline I pulled from a friend's website:

FREE MLM SPONSORING TIPS HOT SHEET™ REVEALS
THE REMARKABLE STRATEGIES & INSIDER SECRETS
TO SPONSORING VIRTUALLY **ANYONE** INTO YOUR
NETWORK MARKETING BUSINESS — AND FILLING
YOUR DOWNLINE WITH SERIOUS BUSINESS BUILDERS

While it's a good headline, it's missing one element: proof.

A statement or claim without proof is just an opinion, and there's no way for the reader to know whether or not it's actually true.

Here's a better version with proof incorporated...

GET SIZZLING HOT MLM SPONSORING TIPS DELIVERED FREE RIGHT TO YOUR INBOX ONCE A WEEK FROM A GUY WHO WENT FROM "MLM FAILURE" TO "INDUSTRY SUPER RECRUITER," SPONSORING 268 PEOPLE IN 12 MONTHS, AND BECAME THE #1 RECRUITER IN HIS COMPANY

The key phrase here is, of course, the proof statement of "Sponsoring 268 people in 12 months."

Use pictures, numbers, and proof of results whenever possible.

Providing proof takes your solution from a dream to reality, but be careful!

Always make sure you follow Federal Trade Commission (FTC) guidelines for best advertising practices and your company's policies. This is especially important if you want to make any kind of personal income claims. Failing to do so could find you on the wrong side of the law or result in the loss of your distributorship.

STEP 5: OFFER A SIMPLE SOLUTION

Once you've established that you have a solution for your prospect, make that solution as simple and easy to acquire and use as possible.

For example:

An e-book is faster and easier to get than a hard copy in the mail.

A "done-for-you" solution is faster and easier than a "do-it-your-self" solution.

Showcase how much work, expense, and effort would go into acquiring the solution the old-fashioned way. Then, showcase how much faster, easier, and less expensive it is to buy yours instead.

STEP 6: REMOVE ALL RISK, AND ADDRESS COMMON QUESTIONS AND OBJECTIONS

By now they should really want to purchase your product or service, but they've got some doubts. Will it work? What if it doesn't? Can I afford it?

If your prospects have common questions or objections, don't pretend they don't exist or ignore them; answer them! Be honest and authentic and put their concerns at ease.

Finally, you want to remove any perceived risks that might be holding them back. This is typically done by offering a money back guarantee…

"You can try XYZ today without any risk at all. If XYZ doesn't meet or exceed your expectations in every way, simply send it back within the next 60 days and we'll immediately issue a full refund."

STEP 7: PROVIDE A CALL TO ACTION

At this point, it's time to tell your prospect exactly what you want them to do next. This is called a "call to action."

An example of a call to action statement would be:

"Getting started is simple. Just click the 'Add to Cart' button now and you'll be taken to our secure checkout page. As soon as you complete the order form, you'll have instant online access to XYZ."

STEP 8: OFFER A BONUS FOR ACTING NOW

If there's still some hesitation left in your prospect's mind, a great way to push them over the edge is to offer a bonus for buying now. This is how you can take your offer from "great" to "irresistible."

Bonuses could be free shipping, additional content, a second bottle of product, your personal time for coaching, or a discount.

The more bonuses you can include, the better your conversions will be. Often, prospects will buy your primary offer just to get the bonuses!

STEP 9: SECOND CALL TO ACTION

After you've offered your bonuses, it's time to give them a second call to action:

"I'm going to include these bonuses at no additional cost, but they're only available on a first-come, first-served basis. Once they're gone, they're gone, so click the 'Add to Cart' button now to get started."

IMPORTANT: DO NOT MAKE FALSE CLAIMS WHEN IT COMES TO THE AVAILABILITY OF YOUR OFFER.

For example, do not say that XYZ is only available at this price for 12 more hours, and then offer that price every single day.

Do not say that your bonuses are limited to the next 20 customers, and then make them available to everyone.

You might make more money in the short run, but making false claims will put you in the category of a scammer and destroy your reputation over the long run. NEVER trade your integrity for money!

STEP 10: PROVIDE THIRD PARTY CREDIBILITY

At this point, it's time to end your presentation with feedback and testimonials from past or current customers. Providing REAL testimonials from real customers will alleviate any lingering doubt that might be left.

Do not make up fake testimonials. That makes you a scammer and a con artist. If you don't have any yet, give your product to a small group of people for free or at a discount in exchange for their honest feedback.

At the end of your testimonials, provide a third and final call to action.

So there you have it!

My 10-Part Formula for creating a $1 million sales presentation.

With that being said, success is in the details...

While this template should give your current marketing efforts an immediate boost, mastering this process will require months and years of continual practice.

Before we move on to the next chapter, I wanted to g
additional tips that will improve your marketing effo

I. USE A SWIPE FILE.

Every single copywriter keeps a swipe file. It's the most important
tool required for the job.

A "swipe file" is a collection of pieces of copywriting that you
save and archive. It is designed to provide you with proven pieces
of sales copy you can use to generate ideas or change to fit your
personal needs.

Anytime I'm surfing the web or flipping through a magazine and
see an ad or sales letter that was written by a well-known copywriter,
I copy and paste the different pieces into my swipe file.

I'll paste the headline into the "Headlines" section of my file, and
then I'll continue to add the rest of the parts to their specific
folder: the subhead, the introduction, the problems, the benefit
bullets, the solution, the close, the guarantee, the P.S., the call to
action, the bonuses, etc.

Anytime I'm starting a new project or get stuck on a current one,
I'll pull out that swipe file and read through it for 30 minutes to
get the ideas flowing and my mindset into copywriting mode.

The fastest way to cure a stint of writer's block is to pull out your
swipe file. I can guarantee that within 10 minutes, you'll find a
sentence or line that will inspire a great new idea or angle for
your letter.

NOTE: **NEVER** USE A PIECE OF COPY WORD-FOR-WORD OR

LINE-FOR-LINE. THAT IS ILLEGAL, **NOT** WHAT A SWIPE FILE IS FOR, AND A VERY QUICK WAY TO MAKE ENEMIES OUT OF VALUABLE INDUSTRY COLLEAGUES.

Use your swipe file to stimulate your own ideas and then put those ideas into your own words.

Creating this file is the single most important thing you can ever do when it comes to writing great copy, so don't skip this vital activity. It can make you a millionaire.

2. YOU GET WHAT YOU ASK FOR.

When it comes to writing your advertisements and marketing pieces, you have to be careful because you'll get exactly what you ask for.

For example, writing ads that promote "quick and easy money or results" tend to get a really high response, which you'll consider a positive result.

Here are two examples of real ads I pulled from Google:

5 × 9 Matrix with Massive Spillover!

Join Today for only $20!

We do all the selling for you!

And...

New Company Launch!

We build one leg for you!

Grab your position now!

They might get a great click-through rate, but think about the quality of those people. Are they going to be leaders? Are they going to show up ready to study a new craft and work years at it?

Heck no.

Ads with that kind of message are going to attract broke, lazy, opportunity junkies.

As my network marketing career developed, I decided to take this lesson learned to the extreme. I had reached a point where I only wanted to work with successful professionals and experienced network marketers.

As a publishing company, *Magnetic Sponsoring* had grown into a full-time occupation, so the amount of time I had to dedicate towards a network marketing opportunity was limited.

Because I knew exactly what kind of people I wanted to work with, I consciously chose an opportunity that would cater to that group. I decided to join a business that sold financial education seminars which took place in exotic locations, and cost about $10,000 to $20,000 each.

The high price of the product automatically excluded time-wasting opportunity junkies from my team and attracted successful people with money who were into investing.

When it came to recruiting, I got even more specific...

I only wanted to recruit a handful of people who were already seeing success in MLM, but they weren't getting paid enough to justify their time and effort.

I wrote a sales letter that I posted online which spoke specifically to this type of person. It acknowledged all of their hard work, but pointed out the small commission checks they were making. Then it offered this company and its compensation plan as the solution to that problem.

Because I was marketing to a very specific group of people, the number of leads I produced was low, but the quality was incredibly high. I only sponsored 15 people, but every single one of them was a self-sufficient leader who built the business full-time. They didn't need me to motivate them, train them, or tell them what to do, which is exactly who I wanted to work with.

The result? Five of them became six-figure earners, and I became the number one residual income earner in the company.

Remember: When it comes to advertising, you'll get exactly what you ask for.

Choose wisely.

3. NEVER TEAR DOWN OTHERS.

I've seen marketers attack other businesses and people in their ads in order to put themselves on a pedestal.

Here are some examples:

DON'T JOIN XYZ UNTIL YOU READ THIS FIRST
FIND OUT THE TRUTH ABOUT THE XYZ SCAM

– Or –

DO YOU LIKE MAGNETIC SPONSORING?
THEN YOU'LL LOVE ABC EVEN MORE

Here's the deal... If what you're marketing can't stand up on its own merits in the marketplace, then you might want to find something else to promote.

Tearing down another person, product, or opportunity for your own financial gain makes you a massive loser. Don't do it.

CHAPTER EIGHT

Becoming a Professional

As I think back over my first four to five years in this industry and evaluate the reasons for my setbacks and successes, one thing becomes very apparent: success came when the emotion left.

When most people first get involved in this industry, they usually do it out of desperation, excitement, or hope. It's an emotional decision.

Unfortunately, the disciplines and skills necessary for success in network marketing are completely foreign to them.

They feel like they've been dropped into a fishbowl and have to sink or swim.

Each lead called is the call of a lifetime.

Each warm market prospect holds the key to their futures.

Each meeting attended contains the secret to success.

Each follow-up call answered by a machine is a shot to the gut.

Every dollar spent on leads is a gamble.

Each call to the upline that's never returned is personal.

The sky starts falling to the ground with every "no."

Every new sign-up is cause for a night on the town.

It's all run on emotion.

And this is why they quit.

This is how I felt my first four years in this industry. It was a complete roller coaster, which always ended in a frustrated, exhausted, and saddened rider.

Honestly, nothing scares me more than the complete jubilation and level 10 enthusiasm of a new rep who couldn't wait to share our product with anyone who had a pulse.

Here's why...

Everything that goes up must come down, and when it comes to emotions surrounding a business, it's a recipe for disaster. People tend to get whipped into an emotional frenzy based on greed and excitement, which creates false expectations. When the pleasure of the oxytocin wears off, and reality sets in, things go bad.

Building a business from the ground up for the very first time is hard. You will experience failure (learning) daily.

And if you are emotionally involved with these learning experiences, they will cause you pain. As a result, you will stop doing the things that caused that pain (such as calling people and being rejected

9 out of 10 times).

At that point, you're finished, unless your "reason why" is big enough and strong enough to push you onward through the pain.

Here's what I want you to know:

True professionals feel no differently about success and failure. They are just part of everyday business and treated as such because they live in a mindset of abundance.

Today, every day is just another day at the office. It's fun. I love what I do, but the emotional highs and lows are gone. In short, I've grown up and into a professional.

I can remember when I lost my number one producer to a sleazy cross-recruiting shark. She'd brought in over half my organization during the first months of my business.

So what did I do about it? Nothing. I didn't lose a wink of sleep. I didn't waste a second wondering why. I didn't whine or complain and I didn't chase after her.

It just didn't matter because I knew where I was going, and that I will get there no matter who comes or goes. There are an endless number of people out there just like her, and even more skilled that I would meet. *My decision to become one of the best in this industry had been made*, so the emotional roller coaster came to an end.

Now it was time to just go to work every day, and treat the good and the bad for what they really are… Just a part of doing business.

The irate calls from customers who forgot they were on auto-ship? Just another day at the office.

The no-shows for follow-ups? Just another day at the office.

The new guy who talks big and then never does jack? Just another day at the office.

The new distributor joining with 1,000 reps from his old company? Just another day at the office.

Keep your emotions out of your day-to-day building. There will be highs and lows daily. If you want to be successful, you can't let them affect you.

CHAPTER NINE

Core Values for Long-Term Success

During my career as an entrepreneur, I've seen dozens of "leaders" come and go in both the network marketing and Internet marketing industries.

They come in, make a big splash, and within 12 months, they're gone.

Why?

There are typically two reasons:

1. They were only in it for the money.
2. They screwed people over to get it.

On the other hand, *Magnetic Sponsoring* has sold more copies than ever, and my most recent business produced more revenue in its first 12 months than *Magnetic Sponsoring* did in its first four years. Why? Because I take a long-term approach to business and taking a long-term approach is everything.

The Internet and social media have changed business forever. In the past, the power was in the hands of the company. If they provided poor service or product quality, you were basically screwed because you were limited to the options within your local area.

Today, companies compete on a global level and the customer has all of the power. This is because their voice and opinion can be heard by thousands of friends and family members with the click of a mouse.

Today we are in a "trust-based economy" where your reputation literally is your business.

Take EVG for example…

I launched EVG in December of 2010 with the clearly stated expectations of: "I'm not an experienced investor, I've made financial mistakes, but we have a big problem and we're going to solve it together."

There are clearly more qualified people to learn from when it comes to investing than I, yet more than 8,600 people joined EVG that very first week…Why? How is that possible?

Did I use some kind of trickery or gimmick? No.

It was possible because I've spent the previous six years building a reputation around the world as someone who is honest, someone who is authentic, and someone who always over-delivers when it comes to the content I provide.

Many who joined EVG did so blindly without even watching the presentation because they've come to trust the products and work that I produce. This kind of loyalty, response, and recommendation would not be possible without sticking to a core set of values.

There is nowhere to hide. If you screw people over today, you won't be in business tomorrow. It's that simple.

Given this fact, it is critically important to create a foundation of values for you and your business right from the start.

With that being said, here are the values that have enabled my success in this business:

1. FORGET ABOUT THE MONEY AND THE MONEY WILL COME

If you do something for money, you will fail. Making money is the byproduct or result of helping other people solve a problem.

When I stopped worrying about making money and started focusing on helping others, the money came quickly and by the truckload.

I do not look for ways to make money. I look for problems I can help people solve.

2. ALWAYS DELIVER WHAT YOU PROMISED, AND ON TIME

If you sell a product to someone, make sure it's delivered quickly. If you say that it will be there in five days, deliver it in three days.

If you're not sure if you can meet a deadline, then don't set one.

3. BE AUTHENTIC

I've been told many times over the years that the reason people like to do business with me is because I'm real. Every event I've ever been to, I'm approached by someone who says, "Wow, Mike, you're exactly the same person in real life as you are on the web."

People don't want to buy from a fast-talking sales person. They want to buy from a friend they can trust.

Be yourself.

4. DELIVER 10 TIMES MORE VALUE THAN THE PRICE

Whenever I produce a product, I make sure it's worth 10 times more than the price.

This is extremely important if it's your very first product and, therefore, your very first impression on your new customers.

5. NEVER MAKE A DECISION BASED ON MONEY

There are extremely profitable products and services that I could promote to EVG Members which would probably make me an extra $50,000 or more per month.

But I don't promote them. Why?

Because in most cases, I don't feel like they're in the best interests of my members. I do what's right for my customers, not what's right for my pocketbook.

It's for this reason that I'll have customers for years, instead of cash for a few months.

6. ALWAYS MAKE DECISIONS FOR THE LONG-TERM

A very good friend of mine recently asked me if I had plans to write a mainstream book based on The Elevation Group (EVG) in the coming months, as it would help with branding and promotion.

I said yes I did, but I'm going to wait at least two or three more years, because I want to earn the right and gather the experience I need to produce a book that can truly change people's lives.

7. WHEN YOU SCREW UP (BECAUSE YOU WILL), ADMIT IT AND APOLOGIZE

While I strive to be the best I can, I am not perfect. Your customers will forgive you and respect you that much more if you acknowledge your mistakes and apologize. Trying to hide it will only turn you into a liar.

8. PROVIDE THE BEST CUSTOMER SERVICE POSSIBLE

Treat your customers as you'd like to be treated. Make it easy to reach your customer service department and train your agents well. They represent you.

9. SAY "THANK YOU" SINCERELY AND OFTEN

If you don't, they will buy from someone else who does.

10. STICK TO YOUR GUNS

Stand up for who you are and your beliefs. You will never be able to please everyone, and attempting to do so will only make you look like a flip-flopping politician. Sticking to your beliefs will help you create true, loyal fans.

11. NEVER BURN A BRIDGE OVER MONEY

I see partnerships or joint ventures fall apart all the time over a financial dispute. Always give the other person the benefit of the doubt and the money that's in question.

It's only dirty paper, and burning a bridge or screwing someone over for money is the quickest way to end up at the bottom.

Industries are small, word gets around, and no one wants to do business with a jackass.

12. NEVER ARGUE WITH A CUSTOMER

Just give them a refund and a respectful "thank you." You don't know what's going on in their life or the problems they may be having. With that being said…

13. FIRE BAD CUSTOMERS

On the other hand, if someone treats you or your team with disrespect, fire them. Give them a refund, remove them from your database, and wish them well. They're never worth the money.

If someone shows up on any of my social media pages and wants to be a jerk, they're banned. If they send a nasty email, unsubscribed and banned. Life's too short to deal with assholes.

14. STAND UP FOR YOURSELF

As you achieve success using the concepts you've learned here in *Magnetic Sponsoring*, you will become a tiny celebrity in your own little way.

While most of the people you have contact with will become fans if you follow the values outlined above, "haters" come with the territory (heck, even Jesus had haters).

Should you find yourself the target of a mentally unstable person who wishes to harm you or your business, stand up for yourself and take the high road. *Do not engage them publically, as they are only looking for attention.*

You can engage them privately to try to find common ground, but understand that what's said in private will likely not stay private, so stick to your values.

When I've seen a negative post in the past, it's usually a case of miscommunication. I'll personally email or call the person to clear the air, and that's worked wonderfully 99 percent of the time.

If they continue to abuse you and your reputation without just cause, get a good attorney and sue the crap out of them.

These people are bullies who feel safe behind a computer. That feeling goes away the moment they're served with a lawsuit in person.

Your reputation is your business. Stand up for yourself.

15. THANK YOUR MENTORS

None of us can build a business or acquire new skills alone. We all need teachers and mentors, and I believe that teaching is the noblest profession in the world.

The single best way to start a relationship with someone you've learned from or look up to, is to let them know how they've made a positive impact on your life.

Send them an email. You'll make their day.

Conclusion

Congratulations, you've officially read *Magnetic Sponsoring* from beginning to end. I hope I've been able to open your mind to some completely new strategies when it comes to building your business.

What I've shared with you today changed my life and has changed the lives of thousands of people around the world. Where you go from here is up to you, but know this:

It doesn't matter where you came from or who you are today...

Your future will be a result of the decisions and actions you make today.

Everything you need to reach your goals is already in you.

I'll say that again:

Everything you need to reach your goals is already in you.

Now go change the world.

I believe in you.

Your brother on the battlefield,

MIKE DILLARD

BONUS TRAINING VIDEO

"What To Do Next..."

I've put together a private video tutorial just
for *Magnetic Sponsoring* book owners that
will help you apply these powerful marketing
strategies in your business as fast as possible.

You can get access to this free training video at:

WWW.MAGNETICSPONSORING.COM/BONUS

Disclaimer and Terms of Use Agreement

The author and publisher of this *Magnetic Sponsoring*™ and the accompanying materials have used their best efforts in preparing *Magnetic Sponsoring*. The author and publisher make no representation or warranties with respect to the accuracy, applicability, fitness, or completeness of the contents of this *Magnetic Sponsoring*. The information contained in this *Magnetic Sponsoring* is strictly for educational purposes. Therefore, if you wish to apply ideas contained in this *Magnetic Sponsoring*, you are taking full responsibility for your actions.

EVERY EFFORT HAS BEEN MADE TO ACCURATELY REPRESENT THIS PRODUCT AND ITS POTENTIAL. EVEN THOUGH THIS INDUSTRY IS ONE OF THE FEW WHERE ONE CAN WRITE THEIR OWN CHECK IN TERMS OF EARNINGS, THERE IS NO GUARANTEE THAT YOU WILL EARN ANY MONEY USING THE TECHNIQUES AND IDEAS IN THESE MATERIALS. EXAMPLES IN THESE MATERIALS ARE NOT TO BE INTERPRETED AS A PROMISE OR GUARANTEE OF EARNINGS. EARNING POTENTIAL IS ENTIRELY DEPENDENT ON THE PERSON USING

OUR PRODUCT, IDEAS, AND TECHNIQUES. WE DO NOT PURPORT THIS AS A "GET RICH SCHEME."

ANY CLAIMS MADE OF ACTUAL EARNINGS OR EXAMPLES OF ACTUAL RESULTS CAN BE VERIFIED UPON REQUEST. YOUR LEVEL OF SUCCESS IN ATTAINING THE RESULTS CLAIMED IN OUR MATERIALS DEPENDS ON THE TIME YOU DEVOTE TO THE PROGRAM, IDEAS, AND TECHNIQUES MENTIONED, YOUR FINANCES, KNOWLEDGE, AND VARIOUS SKILLS. SINCE THESE FACTORS DIFFER ACCORDING TO INDIVIDUALS, WE CANNOT GUARANTEE YOUR SUCCESS OR INCOME LEVEL. NOR ARE WE RESPONSIBLE FOR ANY OF YOUR ACTIONS.

MATERIALS IN OUR PRODUCTS AND OUR WEBSITE MAY CONTAIN INFORMATION THAT INCLUDES OR IS BASED UPON FORWARD-LOOKING STATEMENTS WITHIN THE MEANING OF THE SECURITIES LITIGATION REFORM ACT OF 1995. FORWARD-LOOKING STATEMENTS GIVE OUR EXPECTATIONS OR FORECASTS OF FUTURE EVENTS. YOU CAN IDENTIFY THESE STATEMENTS BY THE FACT THAT THEY DO NOT RELATE STRICTLY TO HISTORICAL OR CURRENT FACTS. THEY USE WORDS SUCH AS "ANTICIPATE," "ESTIMATE," "EXPECT," "PROJECT," "INTEND," "PLAN," "BELIEVE," AND OTHER WORDS AND TERMS OF SIMILAR MEANING IN CONNECTION WITH A DESCRIPTION OF POTENTIAL EARNINGS OR FINANCIAL PERFORMANCE.

ANY AND ALL FORWARD LOOKING STATEMENTS HERE OR ON ANY OF OUR SALES MATERIALS ARE INTENDED TO EXPRESS OUR OPINION OF EARNINGS POTENTIAL. MANY FACTORS WILL BE IMPORTANT IN DETERMINING YOUR ACTUAL RESULTS AND NO GUARANTEES ARE MADE THAT YOU WILL ACHIEVE RESULTS SIMILAR TO OURS OR ANYBODY ELSE'S. IN FACT, NO GUARANTEES ARE MADE THAT YOU WILL ACHIEVE ANY RESULTS FROM OUR IDEAS AND TECHNIQUES IN OUR MATERIAL.

The author and publisher disclaim any warranties (express or implied), merchantability, or fitness for any particular purpose. The author and publisher shall in no event be held liable to any party for any direct, indirect, punitive, special, incidental or other consequential damages arising directly or indirectly.

Testimonial Statements

Mike, I've almost completed the Magnetic Sponsoring book. Wow! I have studied network marketing for a couple of decades and have never found anything close to hitting on all of the keys to success in network marketing - plus providing a system for the old classic challenge of prospecting at the same time. The way the ideas and insights are presented, one can't help but do some serious soul-searching, as well, in terms of facing where the responsibility for success lies.

I will read and re-read Magnetic Sponsoring many times. Your honesty, wisdom, tips, and marketing system are invaluable. The fact that you pull it all together in such a concise way is frosting on the cake.

For anyone who has ever been in network marketing, has been involved but quit, ever entertained the idea of committing to networking as a home-based business, Magnetic Sponsoring is a must read. Thank you for converting your pain, acquired through the school of hard knocks, to the gain of all those who will read this.

TERRI RIFFE, PH.D.

Magnetic Sponsoring is hands down the best "How To..." I have ever read on our industry. After ordering, I couldn't wait to get my hands on it and have read and re-read it multiple times since receiving it. There were many "aha" (I see) moments, that I could relate to.

I highly recommend Magnetic Sponsoring to everyone in the Network Marketing industry, no matter if you are just starting out or you are a seasoned networker.

ILKA FLOOD

Hi Mike,

Read your book this morning.

Just wanted to let you know that you've written the BEST book on the industry that I've ever read, and I've most likely read them all. Magnetic is a classic.

Great job!

MIKE STOKES

It makes a refreshing change to learn how to do something and have the tools to do it. Magnetic Sponsoring has changed the rules! Finally someone is showing us how to do this business and make money from the start. I'll never look at MLM the same way again and I've been around the industry for over 10 years!

DANIEL & HELEN WRIGHT

What Mike Dillard goes over in Magnetic Sponsoring should be considered MANDATORY READING for your downline members and especially for brand new distributors or representatives that you bring into your business. Save yourself a ton of time and agony and get Magnetic Sponsoring into the hands of your partners. When a team member shouts for help just reply by saying "read Magnetic Sponsoring first and we'll take it from there"

KEVIN MALLORY, FOUNDER, THE FORWARD ONLINE GROUP

After being exposed to Magnetic Sponsoring over a month ago, I knew Mike was onto something big. His Magnetic Sponsoring System is taking the network marketing industry by storm. Finally, someone put together a no "BS" strategy that tells it like it really is. This system alone will allow many, many more people to achieve their dream of network marketing success.

After my partner and I teamed up with Mike, within our first 24 hours we had already made over $100 in retail sales. The potential of this powerful system is endless. Bottom line, it works when used correctly.

MICHAEL SHAW & SHERRY CANTUA

Dear Mike,

I have never sponsored any one before, and now after reading Magnetic Sponsoring, only three days ago I have three people in my back office and because of you and your book I had the confidence to phone them. And following your guide on advertising, I am getting visitors! Thank you so much!

SANDRA

Hey Mike... I believe your Magnetic Sponsoring is going to change the way I market online for a long time. I always used to advertise my MLM program first and I would usually spend more in advertising than what I was making per signup in my MLM program.

I started using your suggestions in Magnetic Sponsoring about placing ads on Google AdWords and I also placed the same ad on a free traffic generator.

I just wanted you to know, between the two of them, for the week I have generated almost 77 live, exclusive leads of my own, and have only spent $26 dollars in advertising! I haven't even started picking up the phone yet to build a relationship with the leads I have already generated. I can't wait to see how many I sign up in my MLM program.

Thanks to Magnetic Sponsoring, I can actually get paid to generate leads online instead of losing money for the very first time.

SHANE WOODS

I am a founding member of 3WTel SuperiorVoIP out of Dublin, Ireland. I am currently the top producer in the world for them. I have been marketing for over 20 years and have had my share of ups and downs. I am one of the presenters for the company that does presentations on behalf of all distributors using our new system. Magnetic Sponsoring is amazing...

Simon Taylor, the Director of Sales and Marketing for SuperiorVoiP and myself went to work to create the SV Success System. This system is based solely on the idea of Magnetic Sponsoring. We are now getting the quality people that are focused on starting businesses, not tire-kickers. Magnetic Sponsoring is the best book I've ever read for Networking.

CARL HAAVALDSEN

Hi Mike, I received your book yesterday and I'm absolutely satisfied with what it has to offer I'm not finished reading yet but already I know that my business will not be the same after this!!!

Thanks a lot, I'll keep in touch.

KARLYSON

Just wanted to say thanks for the course and the wonderful insights. I am tweaking my business right now to reflect what you are saying. I think most of the tools are in place, but your attention to detail has shown me a few areas I need to work on.

I sent out the site to a few of my downline to see what would transpire and you will find this amazing (or not)… The very distributors who have a strong business sense are also the only ones who are going through the boot camp and ordering the book.

I guess there are more of the lazy ones involved in our businesses than we think. I have contacted my upline and we are going to make Magnetic Sponsoring part of our training program.

DAN BROOKS

*Magnetic Sponsoring is the best affiliate program I've seen! As you may know, I just received **$4,600** in commissions. Best birthday surprise I've ever had. Thanks for your commitment to sharing this revolutionary material with others.*

ZACH THOMPSON

So I tried returning the Magnetic Sponsoring book and it was returned back to me. I knew that was a sign to read the book. So I read it (shamefully a whole month and a half after my initial receipt) and I finished it in 2 hours.

Not only has the knowledge you shared in the book made me change my whole approach to my business, but it has also made me change my whole daily routine and my usual actions. My biggest downfall was doing what unsuccessful people do… just enough or a little here, a little there, going nowhere. Now I see why my upline is a leader and see how I will become one very soon. Thanks!

SONYA P. COLLINS

Lightning Source UK Ltd.
Milton Keynes UK
UKOW05n0810271114

242252UK00003B/35/P

9 781619 612938